Cinnamon and Salt

Cinna

Salt

non and

Emiko Davies

Hardie Grant

BOOKS

Foreword

The tradition of Venetian *cicchetti* that Emiko writes about so wonderfully in this book is not one made for long, leisurely meals but for a food culture on the move. It is about stopping in for a drink, a snack or a small plate at a hole-in-the-wall bar while walking around the city on the way home from work or while shopping for groceries; it's about pausing to meet friends, do business, exchange news. While it can be brisk, it is inherently sociable. Over an *ombra* of wine and a *cicchetto*, great conversations ensue whether you are perched on a stool or a canal-edge, standing at the bar or walking from one *bàcaro* to the next.

Going out for *cicchetti* is also a surprisingly cheap and unpretentious way to eat and drink in a city that can be eye-wateringly expensive – as I discovered to my great delight when living in Venice as a graduate student researching the city's Renaissance history. Even the fanciest establishments will usually serve you a drink or a coffee and a quick bite at a very reasonable price if you are willing to stand at the bar. A great many paths cross in this way: old ladies in fur coats enjoying a spritz at eleven in the morning; university students on raucous bar crawls; meandering foreigners; and locals in a hurry. The same bars that we frequented during late-night *cicchetti* rounds when we were younger, Emiko and I have returned to more recently, chatting over a drink while our kids played around a shady *campo*.

The evolution of this bar culture is partly a function of Venice's unique topography and its history as one of the largest, most densely populated and cosmopolitan metropolises in pre-modern Europe. The shortage of space to sit and settle in also reflects the anxieties of the aristocratic Renaissance government, who sought to prohibit working-class Venetians from gathering to eat and drink, fearing this would lead to conspiracy, immorality and disorder. At the same time, these authorities acknowledged that wine was a crucial staple, particularly in a city without a good supply of drinking water, and that many people without the space or equipment to cook in their homes would be out looking for a meal.

And so, despite official attempts to control where food and drink establishments were located, what and whom they could serve, a thriving culture of hospitality sprung up in the city in the Middle Ages. A cluster of large centrally located inns (*osterie*) offered more elite international visitors elaborate food, expensive imported wines and comfortable bedrooms upstairs (these evolved into the luxury hotels that welcomed the rising tide of tourists in the eighteenth century). In more peripheral neighbourhoods, humble taverns sold wine – theoretically meant to be taken away and consumed at home – and simple snacks to locals going about their everyday lives. Everywhere, Venetian barkeepers were inventive, managing to carve out a little more space by adding a roof terrace (*altana*) here, or a courtyard there, encroaching onto the surrounding streets and squares and even onto boats moored alongside them on the canals.

All of this was complemented by a vibrant tradition of street food. Wandering pedlars and street stalls sold crabs, oysters, scallops, salted sardines, polenta, tripe, cooked fennel, pumpkin and broad beans, to be eaten on the run, day and night. Their ephemeral presence and street cries were captured in Gaetano Zompini's series of etchings *Le Arti che Vanno per Via* (1746–1754), though many of them could still be seen and heard in the early twentieth century.

The food and drink traditions that survive in Venice's backstreet bars also reflect the city's past as a global crossroads, initially for trade and pilgrimage, later increasingly for tourism, at least since the beginnings of the Grand Tour tradition in the sixteenth century. Located in a strategic position between Europe and the East, Venetians realised early that their fortunes lay in making the city an unavoidable nexus of transit and exchange. Foreigners arriving from every direction were welcomed, as long as they brought something that might benefit the city. Even if Venice also pioneered oppressive forms of control and segregation, most famously with its Jewish ghetto, the mixing of so many people from so many different places in the close confines of the lagoon city inevitably led to creative exchanges, adaptations and inventions. Refugees, foreign merchants and migrant workers brought with them ingredients, tastes and customs that melded together in the crucible of Venetian urban life to produce this 'local' food and drink tradition.

Celebrating and cultivating this tradition of food and sociability, as Emiko does in *Cinnamon and Salt*, can and should be an important part of Venice's recovery after the COVID-19 pandemic, and of making it a vibrant city for residents and visitors into the future. Learning the art of *cicchetti* means exploring the backstreets and lesser-known areas, and encountering some of the city's more obscure histories. Despite the formidable challenges it now faces, Venice at its heart is a model of a sustainable city – since its foundation it has learnt to survive in the midst of difficult environmental conditions and, on more than one occasion, come back to life after plague brought its global traffic to a halt and wiped out large parts of its population.

Whether we visit it in person or virtually through a marvellous book like this, Venice has a great deal to teach us about the pleasures of a life lived on foot (and in boats!); about sustaining strong community traditions and neighbourhood ties while also staying open to the world; about stopping to appreciate quotidian rituals and rhythms and finding beauty in the everyday. Over time, even a disoriented newcomer can learn to navigate the maze of Venice almost like a local, and to recognise which narrow *calle* to duck down to find a favourite place to stop for a drink, a bite and a chat.

Rosa Salzberg, Associate Professor of Italian Renaissance History, University of Warwick

Classici
Classic cicchetti

Moderni
Modern cicchetti

Fritti
Fried cicchetti

Piatti piccoli
Small plates
146

Dolci e bevande
Sweets and drinks
184

Above
Venice as seen from the Giudecca

Right
The Doge's Palace in Piazza San Marco

— Henry James on Venice

'An orange gem resting on a blue glass plate.'

Preface

It doesn't take long for this city to work its magic on me. Just one look at that long, low horizon shaped by the grey-green Venetian waters as the train pulls into the island station, Venezia Santa Lucia, and I find myself breathing a sigh. It never gets old: the lagoon, the water-lapped maze of streets and canals, the salt-worn, crumbling buildings and *campi* (squares) hidden away like secret pockets. Whether enshrouded in winter fog with impending high waters or under the warm, beating sun, Venice is truly unforgettable. Although I have called Tuscany home for fourteen or so years, Venice has long held a place in my heart. I spent four weeks on the island of San Lazzaro as an intern restoring flooded manuscripts and etchings from the Armenian monastery's museum (see the rose petal jam recipe on page 200). Since 2005 I have only missed one Biennale, making the bi-annual visit a ritual. And I find any excuse I can to visit friends in Venice and indulge in *cicchetti*: my very favourite way of eating food (to be honest, it is almost the only way I have ever eaten on countless visits to Venice; I have dined in a proper sit-down restaurant just twice).

The idea for this book wasn't mine. It began, many years ago, at a suggestion by my very good friend Rosa Salzberg, a Renaissance historian from Melbourne who for the past decades has divided her time between Venice, England and her home in Trento. We met by chance about fifteen years ago in Florence, and we connected instantly over cocktails and snacks and, as I recall, we talked all night long, like old friends, which we have become. I often took advantage of her teaching sessions in Venice to pay her a visit and let her guide me through the labyrinth of narrow *calli* to some of her favourite places to eat: the wonderful pastry shop Tonolo, Arco for an *ombra* and *cicchetti* after a wander through the market, Vedova for their legendary fried meatballs, and a drink at the pretty, historic cafe Rosa Salva, which we joke is Rosa's namesake.

During the summer of 2020, in a moment of relative freedom from pandemic restrictions, we met up at our favourite *agriturismo* in Tuscany with our young families, and over bottles of Vernaccia and Chianti and a plate of Cinta Senese *salumi*, Rosa brought up the idea of a book on Venice again and sketched it all out on a napkin (a lot of great things start as 'napkin notes'): 'Food, wine and history in the backstreets of Venice', it read at the top, while underneath in the mind mapping that was carried out were scribbled words like *moscardini, sarde in saor*, cinnamon, Vedova, Timon, *Malvasia*, street food.

I took a photo of the napkin lest it get drowned in wine or used to wipe a toddler's face. We agreed to meet in Venice the next month and spend a weekend fleshing out our napkin. While the children ran around *campi* and back alleys, we drank spritzes and ate at our favourite *bàcari*. Rosa led me around the narrow streets near the Rialto where her research on the history of migration takes her often. I took as many photos as I could while we gathered more ideas. I posted about our weekend full of *cicchetti* and oddly uncrowded canals on Instagram in real time and by the time I got home, on Monday morning, there was an email from my publisher, Jane Willson, who had seen these snapshots of Venice but had no idea I was there gathering ideas for a proposal for her: How about a book on *cicchetti*? It was meant to be.

Introd

uction

— *Giuseppe Maffioli,*
Venetian gastronome and actor

'*Venezia, gazza ladra che prende e porta a casa tutto ciò che luccica o le piace.*'

'Venice, magpie that takes home anything that glitters or that she likes.'

Right
Near the Rialto market

Far Right
Cicchetti at All'Arco

The cuisine of Venice is utterly unique in the Italian peninsula. Refined, yet simple, it has origins that carry the legacy of the Venetian Republic's immense wealth and multicultural influence. Foreign ingredients like sugar from Syria and Egypt, dried fruit, citrus and fried sweets from Persia, spices from India and Indonesia, then later, Norwegian stockfish, corn from Central America and coffee from Turkey, all became part of Venice's indispensable pantry, influenced by the wealthy merchants importing sugar and spices 'who strove to eat food whose signature flavours were anything but local', as John Dickie puts it in *Delizia! The Epic History of the Italians and Their Food* (2007). Yet, at the same time, the cuisine heavily relies on the fresh and excellent but humble ingredients that the lagoon environment and surrounding countryside offer each season, from *moeche* (soft-shell crabs) and tiny grey prawns (shrimp) collected by fishermen, to the delicate artichokes pruned early from the plant while still small, grown on the nearby islands.

This cuisine is a bundle of opposites. It is represented in the opulent Renaissance banquets painted by Veronese and also in the peddlers making vats of polenta or frying sugar-coated fritters on street corners in Gaetano Zompini's eighteenth-century etchings. It is sophisticated but also frugal. This dichotomy, and this history, is partly what makes Venetian food so starkly different to that of the rest of Italy, but it is just the start. Added to it, in rich layers, are also things like the city's unusual topography, the impossible labyrinth of narrow streets and canals that make it a city traversed on foot, that it is an island that lacks fresh water (made up for in wine) and the melting-pot, polyglot, multicultural society of Venice's past that contributed to not only the recipes but also the way people ate and drank, and continue to today.

Venice sits in a shallow inland sea, a network made up of 118 islands connected by about 400 bridges and countless canals. Its elegant *palazzi*, which appear to be impossibly floating on the water, are actually built atop a foundation of wooden piles driven into the mud, often likened to an upside-down forest; it's an urban environment that UNESCO calls an 'architectural masterpiece', carefully linked to its surrounding lagoon ecosystem. Without traffic, other than pedestrians and boats, setting foot in Venice feels like stepping into another time. There are few pockets of green: gardens here and there, a pergola of grapes, but otherwise the green areas for growing food are mainly kept within the walls of ancient monasteries or the outlying islands of the lagoon.

The Venice you see and taste today carries just a whisper of its prosperous and rich maritime and trading past of the Middle Ages, but what you must know about what made Venice so wealthy, what set it apart from the rest of the peninsula and gave it such a prominent place in food history, comes down to one thing: the spices. With an important early salt trade and a prestigious and powerful navy that was even used in the Crusades, Venice collected colonies throughout the Mediterranean, from the Dalmatian coast to Greece and Cyprus. In the twelfth century, the Venetian Republic had so much influence that it was given Byzantine trading privileges with Constantinople, Alexandria in Egypt and Acre in Israel. With this access to the East and an enviable monopoly on precious spices destined for the rest of Europe,

Venice rose to become the wealthiest, most dynamic city in Europe. It traded in cinnamon, pepper, cloves, nutmeg, mace, coriander, saffron and many more spices that, along with sugar – which was just as luxurious – were initially used as medicines.

The young Venetian merchant Marco Polo was one of the first Europeans to travel to China, then under Mongul rule, where he stayed for seventeen years. When he returned to his hometown in 1299, bringing back inspiring tales of China, Tibet, Bengal and Java, where these precious spices came from, he found the city was a heaving marketplace. John Dickie paints this picture: 'By Polo's time, the Rialto hosted the world's most important wholesale market: at that famous bend in the Grand Canal, silks and medicines from the South China Sea could be traded for Flemish cloth and Cornish tin amid a concert of different languages.'

Curious of everything and everyone, the wealthy lagoon city attracted and was attracted to merchants, diplomats, crusaders, bankers, heretics, pilgrims, humanists in exile and migrants from diverse cultures all over the known world, including Armenians, Albanians, Turks ('dining and trading partners rather than enemies', Gillian Riley notes), Syrians, Greeks, Jews and Germans. According to Luisa Bellina and Mimmo Cappellaro in their introduction to the Slow Food book *Ricette di Osterie del Veneto* (1996), a Tuscan would have been considered more of a *forestiero* (a foreigner) than a Syrian, a Turk or a Greek (who made up such a large part of the community that their language crept into the Venetian dialect).

Venice's melting-pot culture was an inevitable source of gastronomical inspiration, lending not only ingredients but also recipes and preparations from abroad. In the Renaissance, in the Castello district, the 'Slavic' quarter of Venice, you would find the bakeries were run by Albanians, while the butchers were Croatian. Armenians taught Venetians how to cook rice (risotto is a great example of the marriage of the lagoon's traditional ingredients with a borrowed ingredient from the East, which became one of the most iconic Venetian dishes; take risotto with peas or quail, the traditional dish to celebrate San Marco, the city's patron saint, every 25th April), as well as how to cultivate produce such as spinach, eggplant (aubergine), quince and melons. The many sauces based on sweetly cooked onions (such as sardines *in saor* and Venetian-style liver), the use of raisins and pine nuts or almonds, or cinnamon, can be traced to the Armenians, whose presence is still important today in Venice in the Armenian monastery on the island of San Lazzaro. In addition, Venice's Jewish community was in itself a melting pot, with residents coming from Spain, Portugal, Turkey, Syria, Tunisia and the Levant. The classic foods from this historic sixteenth-century quarter of Cannaregio (known as the 'ghetto' from the Venetian word *geti*, referring to the nearby metal foundries in this part of the city) are still among Venice's most quintessential dishes.

Also playing a part in Venetian cuisine was the fact that at the height of the Renaissance in 1470, Venice had become the printing capital of the world. Italy's most important aristocratic cookbooks were printed here: Platina's *De honesta volputate et valetudine*, inspired by Maestro Martino da Como's *Liber de arte coquinaria* was published in Venice in 1475 and is considered the first cookbook ever printed; Cristoforo Messisbugo's *Libro novo nel qual si insegna a far d'ogni sorte di vivanda*, printed posthumously in 1564, and the enormous tome of Bartolomeo Scappi, chef to Pope Pius IV and Pope Pius V, known simply as *Opera*, in 1570.

It was a city where cuisines and ideas met, mingled and became diffused. But, by the end of the fifteenth century, Venice's decline in prosperity had begun as Portugal became the new dominant power in international trade. The Plague devastated Venice in 1576 and ravaged it again in 1630, when it lost one-third of its citizens, contributing to its loss of power. However, ever the magpie collecting things it loves, the lagoon city brought in coffee (like the spices centuries before, coffee beans first arrived in Venice's hands from Turkey), which was initially considered to be 'Satan's drink' but was quickly blessed by Pope Clement VIII. Venice opened Europe's very first coffee house in the middle of the seventeenth century, well before Paris or Vienna, and coffee houses remained ever fashionable as important meeting places for socialising and political gatherings (Caffè Florian in Piazza San Marco is a good example; dating to 1720 it is the oldest coffee house in the world and remains practically unchanged in elegance and popularity – every important local and visitor from Casanova to Goethe has passed through its doors).

Around this time, Venice, beautiful and tempting as ever, poised on its lagoon, was considered an important stop on the Grand Tour – the 'locus of decadent Italianate allure', as Bruce Redford calls the city in *Venice and the Grand Tour* (1996) – and it was considered one of the most refined and elegant cities of Europe. *La Serenissima*, as the 'Most Serene' Venetian Republic was known, lasted an impressive eleven centuries, from 697 to 1797, when it was split into French and Austrian states (and even here she found inspiration in Austrian desserts and drinks – the spritz, that most famous Venetian tipple, comes from the Austrian spritzer). Venice finally became part of the recently unified Italy in 1866.

Above
Strolling the Riva degli Schiavoni, the historical port for merchant ships (named for the merchants from the Dalmatian coast, which was known as 'Schiavonia' during the times of La Serenissima, and today as Montenegro and Croatia)

Left
Piazza San Marco

Introduction

A medieval spice emporium

The link between East and West left an undeniable mark on Venice's cuisine, making it unique in Italy's regions. While food historian and adopted Venetian Carla Coco talks of 'Rivers of spices, kilos of sugar, gold leaf on oysters and rice' to entertain and seduce important foreign dignitaries in Renaissance Venice, Gillian Riley in *The Oxford Companion to Italian Food* points out that the spices were still used carefully and sparingly, and asserts that they 'did not fall in a cloud over every dish', reflecting the expense of the precious ingredients – it's worth noting that the word 'spices', *spezie*, comes from Latin, meaning 'special goods'.

The Venetians were master entrepreneurs, however, creating *sachetti veneziani*, 'little Venetian sacks', of specially mixed spices in different formats to sell to the rest of Europe: *dolce*, mild (for fish, especially), or *forte*, spicy, (better for meat and especially game, a universal spice mix of pepper, cinnamon, ginger, cloves and saffron). In the *Libro per Cuoco* (literally, 'Book for Cook'), one of the earliest complete recipe manuscripts, written by an 'anonymous Venetian' cook in the mid-fourteenth century, about three-quarters of the recipes call for spices. Recipe seventy-four is for a *dolce* spice mix, which includes cinnamon, cloves, ginger and mace.

What was the appeal of these extraordinarily expensive spices? They're not necessary for survival – the idea that spices were used to preserve or disguise the taste of old or bad meat has long been put to rest by food historians. Salt is much more useful for preservation and in the Middle Ages was not nearly as expensive, and – as Riley noted – spices in recipes were actually used sparingly. So, where did the demand come from? Journalist Giampiero Rorato in *Spezie, Vino, Pane della Serenissima* explains that spices were considered valuable because of their high price and therefore became a symbol of one's status. There was enormous request among the aristocrats of Europe for the aptly named 'special goods', in particular for their medicinal, cosmetic and pharmaceutical value. 'Luxury in Europe fed itself in Venice', wrote Venetian gastronome Giuseppe Maffioli.

That so many of these spices helped in the digestion department – everything from ginger to cinnamon to clove and anise all have digestive properties – meant their appearance in the kitchen was only natural, suggests Rorato. Indeed, the idea of tempering illness or discomfort in the body and mind by balancing the four humours (which were related to the elements of earth, air, fire and water, as well as the seasons and stages of life) dates to ancient Rome and was well followed in the Middle Ages. Medieval doctors recommended Asian spices, which had naturally hot and dry qualities to balance out 'cold' and 'wet' European foods.

The move away from strong spices happened in the seventeenth century. John Dickie argues that the use of spices recounted in *Libro per Cuoco* was not so much particularly *Venetian* as it was *medieval*. But there is one spice that continues to appear in the most traditional Venetian cooking: cinnamon. Used in savoury rather than sweet dishes, it will often appear in *agrodolce*, or sweet-and-sour recipes, with stewed meat or fish (see the *Baccalà al pomodoro*, page 170, for example), and in sausages or preserved meats. According to Slow Food, up until as recently as the 1970s (some blame the omnipresent tomato for pushing spices into disuse today), every Venetian pantry had a precious collection of finely ground cinnamon, nutmeg and cloves, and it was not out of place to find cinnamon and sugar on trattoria tables as condiments. You can still imagine it easily with a humble dish of gnocchi *alla veneziana*, 'Venetian-style gnocchi', where potato dumplings are seasoned with sugar, cinnamon and parmesan cheese, a recipe today quite unchanged from when it appeared in Messisbugo's sixteenth-century cookbook.

Renaissance feasts

It doesn't really take too much effort to imagine how the long and incredible history of Venice has left its mark on the cuisine today. A glance at some Venetian paintings from the sixteenth century lets us in on the food, its plating and how it was served and eaten at the time – and there are some similarities that haven't changed much today.

Veronese's *Wedding Feast at Cana* (1563) is a glorious (and huge! It is almost 10 metres/32 feet long) and quite raucous depiction of an aristocratic banquet portraying the biblical story where Jesus, arriving at a wedding where there was nothing left but water to drink, turns the water into wine. It was commissioned by the Benedictine monks for the refectory wall of the Basilica di San Giorgio Maggiore, with its brilliant white marble Palladio facade that faces Piazza San Marco where the Grand Canal opens into the lagoon. The sumptuous feast is represented in full sixteenth-century Venetian style and contains more than 130 immaculately dressed figures. Guests are seated at the table with countless plates of candied fruit, sugar-coated nuts, quince paste and, of course, wine. On the upper levels, roast birds are being prepared – chopped, plated and passed along – while in the foreground wine is being poured from enormous, decorative stone vessels. There is a real buzz in this scene; you can almost hear the noise, the chatter, as wine is being distributed

rather urgently by busy servants. It might be a patrician banquet, but you could imagine the same kind of clamour in a Renaissance *osteria*.

Venetian painter Leandro Bassano's canvas of the same scene (1579–1582) is a relatively simple and less opulent event set in a *palazzo* in the Venetian countryside. The guests sit around a single table which, rather than being covered with platters of food, contains a plate of large, plump prawns (shrimp), a single roast bird (perhaps duck; there are others hanging above the table), a loaf of bread set directly on the tablecloth and a glass carafe of white wine (interestingly, my sommelier husband, Marco, thinks this sixteenth-century white looks like an orange wine, in other words a white wine that has been macerated with skins on that lends the wine an amber glow and gives it a bit more body – a traditional way of making white wine in this area, being brought back to the Venetian lagoon in places like Venissa: see page 87).

The details of the kitchen are wonderful too, as they show you the prime ingredients: gleaming silver sea bass in a corner, and fruit and vegetables (from all seasons) together in the other corner – winter radicchio, summer apricots and peaches, a bursting pomegranate from autumn and spring's spiny artichokes. Above the basket, a young servant is about to carry out a large, shallow basket full of *Bussolai* (page 210), the S- and ring-shaped biscuits beloved by Venetians. Fresh prawns (shrimp), roast duck and *bussolai* washed down with white wine sounds more or less like an ideal, special Venetian meal today too.

Veronese later painted another fantastic banquet known as *Feast in the House of Levi* (1573), where sixteenth-century aristocratic Venetians are depicted in another lively scene centred around the table. Never mind the storyline (originally it was meant to depict the Last Supper, but when Veronese was summoned by the Venetian Inquisition and interrogated about the overly lavish setting and 'inappropriate' characters, 'buffoons, drunken Germans, dwarfs and other such scurrilities', according to the manuscript of the hearing, he simply changed the title), we are too busy looking at the details of this feast. Servants pour wine out of beautiful rounded glass decanters, small plates of food are passed around and guests carry long toothpicks – they were usually perfumed – for picking up sticky candied fruit. A young soldier on a staircase, his weapon leaning against his body to free his hands, appears to be chatting to a fellow soldier (presumably these are the 'drunken Germans'). He is holding a small plate of morsels of food in one hand while the other holds a glass of wine up to his lips. It's not a far stretch to place them on a bridge over a canal and think they're enjoying *cicchetti* at aperitivo hour.

Bartolomeo Scappi's cookbook *Opera* was published in Venice right around the same time as Bassano's painting and Veronese's noisy banquet scenes, so it's not hard to imagine how Scappi's banquets may have looked. Typical was a sequence of 136 dishes over seventeen courses and, as Gillian Riley says of this succession of these Renaissance dishes, 'Perhaps one should think of them as "tapas" – when a group share exquisite small portions of many things, sipping drinks and chatting.' Or – if I may – not tapas but, strictly and uniquely, *cicchetti*.

Before you Start

Measurements

I always measure recipe ingredients by metric weight (with the occasional handful or pinch, by eye, by feel or by taste). It is the way Italians cook and it is the most reliable way to measure out ingredients in a recipe. I thoroughly suggest doing the same for best results, particularly for baking. Cups and spoons is where it gets a little more confusing, so please bear with me here: I use a 20 ml (¾ fl oz) tablespoon measurement. If using a 15 ml (½ fl oz) US tablespoon, just be a tad more generous – the 5 ml (⅛ fl oz) difference would be a teaspoon worth. I have also measured cups where applicable with Australian (Commonwealth) cups, i.e., a 250 ml (8½ fl oz) cup, not a 236 ml (8 fl oz) US cup so, if using US cups, again, be on the slightly generous side (the difference, 14 ml/½ fl oz, is almost the equivalent of a tablespoon, so in many cases this won't make a huge difference, but if you want to be precise, add an extra level tablespoon; for 125 ml/4 fl oz/½ cup, add half a tablespoon and so on). When measuring dry ingredients with cups, use this technique: heap the ingredients into the cup with a spoon or scoop (perhaps over a bowl to catch and save the excess), then level off with the back of a knife. For ingredients such as sultanas or nuts, use an unpacked, level cup.

Cooking times

Recipes were tested on an induction cooktop and a conventional oven. You may need to adjust cooking times slightly for gas or electric cooktops and, if baking with a fan-forced oven, which can be hotter, you should decrease the temperature by 20°C (35°F) to be closer to a conventional oven temperature. Cooking times can also vary depending on the type of cookware you use – food will behave differently in a non-stick pan versus a cast-iron pan, for example, but use these times as an indication and note the sensory cues mentioned too.

Frying

See pages 118–121 for all my tips on frying, from oil type to temperature to how to dispose of frying oil.

Servings

Cicchetti are at the heart of this book – small bites of food, often finger food. But sometimes these dishes can be made as main dishes or as part of a bigger meal. Most often, I've given serving sizes for cicchetti, which are, say, one small crostino or a halved hard-boiled egg, and are normally eaten together with many other cicchetti and enjoyed as aperitivo, before a meal, but can sometimes take the place of a light meal.

Crostini

The perfect base for turning practically anything into *cicchetti*, crostini are toasted rounds of bread or firm polenta, cut into square or rectangular slices. I like to toast them on a very hot cast-iron griddle plate to get those nice grill marks. Any pan will do though, just toast until they begin to warm and brown on one side then flip them over and toast the other side (see page 50 for making polenta crostini). I prefer this to oven-toasting or the toaster, which tends to dry out the bread completely, making them a bit too crunchy.

Eggs

Where possible, use free-range, organic eggs that are approximately 55 g (2 oz), which would correspond to large eggs in the US, Canada and Australia, and medium eggs in Europe. If using larger eggs, you will need to adjust the timing on things such as the hard-boiled eggs, which can take 12 minutes to cook instead of 9 (see page 77).

Flour

In Italy, the flour most commonly used is *grano tenero tipo 00*, which is soft wheat, very finely ground – type '00' indicates how finely the flour is ground rather than protein value. It can be replaced with plain (all-purpose) flour. For baking recipes that call for flour with the addition of baking powder, which you will find in the *Pevarini* (page 217) and Zaira's fruit cake (page 222), you could try to replace the amount of flour with self-raising flour and eliminate the baking powder, but the results may be slightly different. In the biscuits, you don't need as much lift as the heavier fruitcake, for example. I personally prefer using plain (all-purpose) flour with baking powder added to it because I can control how much lift (in other words baking powder) I want in it, and I can also ensure that the baking powder I am using is very fresh; it does not keep as well as flour does. In Italy, where I live, self-raising flour is not used, so it is also a question of what I have available, as well as the above practical reasons.

Garlic

I highly recommend smelling the individual garlic clove before using it. It should not smell at all dusty or mouldy, but if it does, discard it and try another – that smell is very difficult to hide later, especially in these Venetian dishes where garlic is often liberally scattered at the end of preparing a dish, when it is at its most pungent. When you have slightly older cloves of garlic lying around, in Italy it's common to split the clove in half lengthways and remove the green sprout, if present; it is said to be bitter and indigestible.

Olive oil

I only use extra-virgin olive oil for both cooking and dressing – although I have a slightly more special, unfiltered extra-virgin olive oil that I keep just for dressing and finishing dishes. In the case of deep-frying, you can use a 'light' (i.e. refined) olive oil or another vegetable oil, such as sunflower oil, which would be the best option (see pages 118–121 for more on frying).

Parsley

When I say parsley, I mean the large, flat-leaf kind, and it should be minced very finely, along with the garlic, and sometimes, if needed, with a pinch of salt – chop it all on the same board together. When added, often along with olive oil, this is the very tasty, classic finish to any Venetian dish.

Polenta

In the Veneto, a very fine-ground pale yellow polenta (cornmeal) is often used. If you can, choose the 'fioretto' kind. White polenta is often used to pair with seafood. If you can, seek out the Biancoperla variety. See page 50 for details on how to prepare it and on portion sizes.

Preserved fish

There is a long history of using preserved fish in this region of Italy. *Baccalà* is, confusingly, the term used for both air-dried stockfish and salt cod in the Veneto. See page 42 for more on dried stockfish, its storage and how to prepare it, and page 136 for salt cod. Also used in this region is smoked herring (see page 156), and don't forget tinned fish (page 103).

Salt

I use sea salt for cooking (fine sea salt for most dishes and coarse salt for salting water for pasta or curing fish, for example). Be aware that using kosher salt or table salt can produce very different results – in general, table salt is less salty than sea salt and kosher salt can vary in saltiness between brands. I recommend wherever and whenever you can, taste as you go.

Sugar

Mostly regular granulated sugar is called for in these recipes, but occasionally caster (superfine) sugar is useful, especially in a cocktail like the Bellini (page 193), where it dissolves quickly, or in the delicate, buttery *Bussolai*, S- and ring-shaped biscuits (page 210). If you don't have it, you can place your regular sugar in the food processor and give it a bit of a whizz. A very clean coffee grinder can do the same.

Fresh and frozen food

Where possible, shellfish should be extremely fresh, even live in the case of razor clams, or *schie* and *moeche* crabs that are eaten whole. If you can only get frozen seafood, some very good options are the octopus recipes, which benefit from being frozen (freezing octopus is a form of tenderising), or cuttlefish/calamari. Always choose the most sustainable local option. This might include foregoing a more convenient option but, in some places, some forms of fishing – for example, trawling for very small prawns (shrimp) (see page 140 for *schie*) – mean the nets used are very tight and not the most sustainable option.

Octopus at the Rialto market

Classici
Classici
Classici
Classici
Classici

Classici
Classic cicchetti

Baccalà mantecato
Whipped cod

Polenta in due modi
Polenta, two ways

Baccalà alla Vicentina
Vicenza-style baccalà

Sarde in saor
Sweet-and-sour fried sardines

Radicchio in saor
Sweet-and-sour radicchio

Fondi di articiocchi
Artichoke bottoms

Scampi grigliati
Grilled scampi

Moscardini col sedano
Baby octopus with celery

Polpi in tecia
Octopus in wine

Seppie con piselli
Stewed cuttlefish with peas

Patatine condite
Dressed new potatoes

Uova sode in vari modi
Boiled eggs, a few ways

'Venice knows about
aperitivo. How
to do it well and
even make a small
occasion of it … like
everything else.'

Right
Vino Vero in Cannaregio

What are cicchetti?

Cicchetti (pronounced chi-ke-tee and also spelled *cicheti* in Venetian dialect) are a way of life in Venice. The word comes from the Latin *ciccus*, meaning 'small thing'. Think of these morsels as appetisers, aperitivo, hors d'oeuvres, or (if you must) compare them to Spanish tapas (which get their name from the word *tapa*, meaning 'to cover', as these morsels began as a slice of ham draped over a glass of wine to keep flies out), but *cicchetti* are undeniably, distinctly Venetian, with rich history behind them.

Served in *bàcari*, *cicchetti* are generally small enough to be eaten in one or two bites. You can hold them with one hand while the other holds a spritz, the classic, jewel-toned aperitif of Venice, or an *ombra*, 'a shadow' – a little, rounded glass of wine, just enough for a few mouthfuls, named after the shadow of Piazza San Marco's lean bell tower that wine sellers used to follow to keep their wine cool.

Eating *cicchetti*, perhaps leaning on a stone counter or perched by the bridge of a canal, and hopping from one *bàcaro* to the next for a bite before wandering home, has long been an economical way to socialise and is so suited to the casual Venetian way of life, which is largely on foot. It's also not only an evening thing; you'll find some of the most traditional *bàcari* hold opening hours that allow market sellers or goers to stop in for breakfast and last-calls just before dinner. Do Mori (see page 85), which has been in operation since 1462, opens at 8 am and closes at 7.30 pm, for example; all they sell is wine and *cicchetti* to go with it.

Typical *cicchetti* include both warm and cold dishes, plenty of seafood – which the lagoon city is known for – and also meat, eggs, *salumi* and vegetables. Creamy whipped cod, known as *baccalà mantecato*, served on crisp-fried polenta crostini or slices of baguette, is a must, and just-out-of-the-kitchen, too-hot-to-hold, juicy *polpette di carne* (crumbed and fried meatballs) are always worth

lining up for. Take your pick from the counter line-up of deep-fried and battered calamari, *folpetti* or boiled baby octopus, crostini layered with punchy pickles and gorgonzola or prosciutto, large grilled prawns (shrimp) or scampi served with a puddle of soft white polenta, simple halves of hard-boiled eggs topped with an anchovy, or boiled artichoke bottoms that you can pick up with a toothpick.

When I asked some Venetian friends for their favourite *cicchetti,* I got similar answers. 'I start with *baccalà mantecato*', said Manuel Bognolo, a crab fisherman on the Giudecca (see page 138), whose go-to *bàcaro* is Cantinone Già Schiavi. My Renaissance historian friend Rosa Salzberg agreed, though her ideal place for it is 'in one of the low-lit bars on the *fondamenta* in Cannaregio on a cold evening'. Edoardo Gamba, a Venetian architect, expands his favourite *cicchetto* situation because, to him, 'It coincides almost always with a moment of rest and *ciacoe* (chatting), which signals that it is mid-Saturday morning. As this often happens while towing the shopping from the Rialto market or a visit to Mascari (a wine shop near the Rialto), my *cicchetto* has the appearance and taste of the crostino with gorgonzola and anchovies of Arco, obviously accompanied with a red *ombra*.'

My personal favourite *cicchetto* is *sarde in saor*: fried fresh sardine fillets marinated in softly cooked white onions and doused with vinegar, raisins and pine nuts – preferably prepared the day before serving. It's a delicious, reviving sweet-and-sour dish that is relatively unchanged from Venetian recipe books of the 1300s. Venetians will prepare many things *in saor*, from grilled slices of eggplant (aubergine) or wedges of radicchio to fried pumpkin, scampi or other types of fish. Without refrigeration, the technique of marinating fried food in vinegar was a well-used method of conservation for Venetian fishermen and merchants.

Cicchetti, spritz, Prosecco, Bellini

Classic *cicchetti*

How to make the ideal cicchetti

There is a tongue-in-cheek piece that both made me smile and gave me a lightbulb moment in Venetian journalist Sandro Brandolisio's book on *cicchetti* of the 1950s and 60s (*Cichéti: Ricettario dei cichéti preparati nei 'Bàcari' veneziani negli anni '50–'60*), where he describes the important tips for making *cicchetti* from the point of view of the *bàcaro* host: make them salty, make them spicy or make them hard to swallow, so you entice customers to drink more wine.

The classic *goto* (a small tumbler that holds about 125 ml/4 fl oz/½ cup of liquid), or *ombra* (glass of wine) in a Venetian wine bar is much smaller than a standard glass, and they are cheap too, as are the *cicchetti*, which usually range from 1–2 euro each. A crostino with gorgonzola, writes Brandolisio, guarantees at least three drinks!

The lightbulb moment was that thanks to these enterprising hosts in the 1950s, some of the most classic *cicchetti* that you will be guaranteed to find today include a crostino smeared with gorgonzola, or anything with an anchovy on it, especially half a boiled egg. Boiled eggs in general are a must, and if you've ever tried to eat a hard-boiled egg without washing it down with something

after, you'll see why things that are hard to swallow without a drink are a classic type of *cicchetto*. Think *polpette* of all kinds and boiled new baby potatoes, too. One of my favourite *bàcari* serves simple roasted potatoes, strung on a skewer, heavy on the salt. They're moreish and they do require that you order another *ombra* afterwards.

I would add that because eating *cicchetti* usually involves standing rather than sitting, and perhaps balancing a plate on the edge of a canal with one hand holding a drink, you need to ensure that you only need one hand to eat with. So, consider serving your *cicchetti* on a stick, such as a skewer or a toothpick. It used to be that large plates, platters, or even pots were placed directly on the counter and customers would use a toothpick to fish out the morsels, be it a baby octopus or artichoke bottoms. Toothpicks are a great way to ensure that nothing slides off too, especially, say, atop an egg. Otherwise, be aware to craft your *cicchetti* with enough of something to help things stick – think mayonnaise or a soft cheese (gorgonzola ticks all the boxes, or ricotta or mascarpone for something more delicate) – whatever will ensure that when lifting the *cicchetto* to your mouth the topping will not tumble.

Opposite are some of the most classic *cicchetti* that make up part of the offerings you can find in Venice. They are so simple to assemble they don't really need a recipe, but they shouldn't be missing from a great *cicchetti* spread. Serve these combinations on a crostino of your choice – toasted or untoasted slices of bread or baguette, or rectangles of fried polenta (see page 50) – or even inside a small bun, like the perfect mortadella panini they do at Al Mercà. Remember to insert a toothpick in the round things that may roll off.

- Gorgonzola with an anchovy

- Half a boiled egg (see page 77) with an anchovy

- Gorgonzola with half a juicy fig

- A slice of prosciutto, a ball of melon and a torn piece of buffalo mozzarella or burrata, or blob of ricotta

- A halved cherry tomato, a paper-thin slice of lardo and ricotta

- A slice (or thick wedge) of mortadella and a pickled long, green pepper

- A slice of Asiago with a smear of mostarda (spicy, nose-tingling fruit compote – try chutney instead)

- Prosciutto cotto or ham with black olive pâté

- Marinated eggplants (aubergines) (see page 92) with mozzarella

- A slice of *salame* with giardiniera pickles

- Ricotta with semi-sundried tomatoes

- Grilled sausage on polenta

- Cheese, of any kind, but especially aged ones such as large chunks of parmesan, pecorino or provolone piccante

A water-lapped door

The Rio della Misericordia in Cannaregio

Baccalà versus stockfish and the shipwreck discovery of a Venetian staple

BACCALÀ IS A POPULAR, traditional ingredient found on tables all over the Italian peninsula, although it originally comes from Norway. The Italian term *baccalà* usually refers to fillets of Atlantic cod (and sometimes Pacific cod) preserved under salt with or without the additional process of drying, while Atlantic cod that has only been air-dried without salt is known as *stoccafisso*, stockfish – the latter is only produced on Lofoten archipelago in Norway still today and is one of the most ancient forms of preserved fish. The Venetians, however, confusingly, call the dried, unsalted stockfish *baccalà*. The confusion might be explained with some etymology: *stoccafisso*, or stockfish, comes from the Middle Dutch *stoc*, 'stick', and *visch*, 'fish', referring to the wooden frames where the cod is dried, while *baccalà* comes via the Spanish (who lent some of their vocabulary to the Serenissima while they were in control of a large part of not-far-away Lombardy from 1535 to 1707) from the Latin *baculus*, or 'stick'.

Baccalà is a protagonist in Venetian cuisine. How this dried delicacy came to the lagoon from the polar north is an incredible story, and one of my favourites in Venetian food history. Carla Coco in her book *Venezia in Cucina* (2007) tells it as a riveting tale of shipwreck and adventure after Venetian captain Piero Querini's planned trip to Bruges, in Flanders, goes terribly wrong.

It is 3rd February, 1432, ten months after setting sail from Crete with a ship full of Malvasia, cypress wood, pepper, ginger and cotton. After living off rancid cheese and *panbiscotto* (hardy crackers produced in the communal ovens of the Serenissima), Querini finds himself and what is left of his freezing, starving crew on the Norwegian island of Røst on the archipelago of Lofoten, where they turn to a diet of limpets foraged off rocks for a month until they are saved by local fishermen (of the sixty-eight sailors that set sail, eleven, including Querini, are left, adds Giampero Rorato in *Origini e Storia della Cucina Veneziana*). They spend more than 100 days on the island being taken care of and waiting for the warmer weather. Querini describes this time as like being on the 'sphere of paradise', quite likely for the habits of the local women who freely go nude to the saunas, which he recounts enthusiastically.

During this time Querini also takes many notes of the techniques of conserving cod – *stocfisi*, he calls the fish – it is dried in the wind and sun without salt, becoming as hard as wood. 'When they want to eat them, they beat them with the flat side of an axe until they are frayed, like nerves, then they add butter and spices to add flavour.' He recounts, too, how the stockfish is used to barter other goods, from iron to legumes, in place of money. Before heading back to Venice he leaves his island saviours with a set of six Venetian silver cups, spoons and forks (the latter of which was extremely rare at the time) and, in return, is given a focaccia, three large loaves of rye bread and sixty stockfish, which are used to barter other goods on their long journey home. They finally return to Venice on 24th January, 1433.

Coco points out that although Querini doesn't ever mention it in his documentation of his journey, we might assume that some of those sixty stockfish must have arrived safely in Venice with him. But for the lagoon city, rich with fresh seafood, it takes at least another century before stockfish appears in regular registers noted by the church, when the appearance of a well-conserved, readily available ingredient like stockfish would have been the ideal candidate for lean-eating days (every Friday, plus Lent and other holy days, a total of around 150 days where eating meat was prohibited). In fact, one of the very first recipes for stockfish to appear in Italy was in Bartolomeo Scappi's *Opera* from 1570. The chef to Pope Pius IV and Pope Pius V, he describes the beating of *merluccie secche* (dried cod) to tenderise it, and long soaking before cooking in a stew with onions and spices (pepper, cinnamon and cloves are mentioned), or frying pieces dusted in flour and serving with a bitter orange sauce.

Today, stockfish is usually sold whole, minus the head, and being completely dried it is as hard as a rock (more on that in a moment), while salted *baccalà* comes already cut into fillets, and both need plenty of time soaking in fresh water to become tender (in the case of stockfish) and palatable (as with salted *baccalà*) before use.

As stockfish is incredibly hard and sold whole, it is not easy to prepare at home – and it is also expensive considering the drying process reduces the fish by 80 per cent of its original weight; it fetches prices nearly double that of a good T-bone steak for the highest-quality stockfish, so you do not want to waste any of it! One trick to its preparation in the Veneto is that it is beaten to tenderise it a little to cut down on soaking time. There is an ancient, dedicated spot for beating *baccalà* on two short stone columns by the Ponte alle Guglie where, today, you will find a gondola parked. You need a few people to help do it; one would sit on a chair to the side and hold the fish over the column, while two others, the '*bati baccalà*', or '*baccalà* beaters', standing, would take turns beating it with a huge wooden mallet. Sometimes this was done on the marble fountains found in various *campi*. Elizabeth David, in her book *Italian Food*, published in 1954, writes, 'The bashing of the *baccalà* along the canals

and in the marketplace is a familiar sight.' Later, mechanical beating, known as *battitura della baccalà*, could do this more quickly and in larger quantities.

Why all the energy to do this? It can take 7–12 days of soaking, changing the water every 8 hours, to revive and tenderise the fish, and the smell can become quite strong even when changing the water frequently – ideally, you want to keep it in the fridge as you do this, which involves finding space as well as the right container to keep it all submerged. In Italy, you can ask your trusted delicatessen to soak it for you (they have special basins with constant running cold water for this) so you only need to order it and pick it up a week later, ready to cook, which is ideal. You can also use pre-soaked salted cod, but be aware that it has a significantly different flavour and texture than stockfish and is not the same thing, so is not always exactly interchangeable in recipes. In Venice, the place to visit is the Rialto market, where you can buy it from any of the fishmongers, already soaked, or the old-school neighbourhood shop Gastronomia Ortis in the Castello district, where they still soak *baccalà* in wooden *tinozze*, barrels, next to a stack of Coca-Cola bottles. (See page 226 for a list of places to find stockfish and *baccalà* internationally.)

Whipped cod

Baccalà mantecato

YOU CANNOT TALK ABOUT Venetian *cicchetti* without mentioning *baccalà mantecato*. Dried cod, soaked, poached and whipped into an elegant mousse, spread on a slice of baguette or, more traditionally, grilled polenta, it's an obligatory taste of Venice. In *The Oxford Companion to Italian Food*, Gillian Riley compares it to France's *brandade de morue*, but adds, 'Patriots and purists see the Venetian recipe as superior in every way.'

Ready-made *baccalà mantecato* has become easily available and even the fishmongers in the Rialto market sell it vacuum-packed, ready to take home and spread onto crostini. One wonders if Venetians bother making this at home anymore, but this is actually quite an easy preparation, especially with pre-soaked cod ordered from the deli (see *Baccalà* versus stockfish and the shipwreck discovery of a Venetian staple, page 42). Like all good but very simple recipes, you need the right ingredients. To start with, you need the right fish: stockfish, not salted cod but the dried, unsalted kind (see page 42).

The key to making this dish is in the Italian verb, *mantecare*, which comes from the Spanish word for butter and means 'to cream'. In fact, the technique for making a successful *baccalà mantecato* is much like that for making mayonnaise: a dribble of olive oil at a time with one hand, while the other beats like mad with a wooden spoon. Recipes from Venetian Jewish kitchens might add some milk to the poaching liquid, which adds to the creaminess.

NOTE If you cannot get pre-soaked dried stockfish or ask your local delicatessen to do it, you have two options: you could substitute with salted *baccalà* which, although not quite the same, needs to be soaked to remove the excess salt; cover with fresh water and keep in the fridge for 48–72 hours, changing the water every 8 hours before using. I recommend tasting a small piece to decide if it is ready. Be aware that the tail end/thinner parts of the fish will be saltier than the thicker parts. Otherwise, you can soak the stockfish yourself. To do this you need to find a container large enough to fit the whole stockfish in your fridge, ideally with a lid to keep odours at bay. Change the water after the first 2 hours. Then it takes a further 7–12 days of soaking, changing the water twice a day at least. Pounding the fish with a meat pounder or wooden mallet can help to tenderise it, and you may need to do this to separate the fish into pieces to make it fit conveniently. Some suggest boiling for 10 minutes (the limitation here is the size of your pot and the length of the fish) after an initial 1-hour soak and a good beating with a mallet to soften it enough to cut, then soaking as described. What you are looking for is complete rehydration of the fish. It should be firm but not rock hard; you will be able to cut it fairly easily and it should no longer have a woody appearance.

Those who like it with a kick might like to stir in some finely chopped raw garlic at the end of this recipe. You may also like to add some chopped parsley and freshly grated nutmeg to serve.

*Makes approx. 500–600 g
(1 lb 2 oz–1 lb 5 oz/2 cups)*

700 g (1 lb 9 oz) pre-soaked baccalà
    (unsalted dried stockfish)
2 garlic cloves
1 bay leaf
125 ml (4 fl oz/½ cup) extra-virgin olive oil
white pepper, to taste
sliced baguette or grilled white polenta,
    to serve

Place the soaked baccalà in a large saucepan with the garlic and bay leaf and cover with cold water. Add a good pinch of salt (please be careful about this if using salted cod, though; you may prefer to wait until the end to add salt to taste). Bring to the boil and simmer for 15 minutes, or until the fish flakes easily (test a corner of the fish with a fork). Drain the fish, reserving a little of the water for later. Remove the garlic cloves (if you like you can add these to the baccalà) and bay leaf, and carefully remove and discard the skin and any large bones – it will be very hot.

Break the fish into pieces and place in a bowl (or your mixer fitted with the balloon whisk attachment, although note that using a food processor will result in a different, creamier consistency – purists will shake their heads at the thought of a metal blade doing the work). Then, while

the fish is still quite warm, begin whipping or pounding to 'cream' the fish with a wooden spoon. At the same time, add the olive oil in a thin, slow drizzle, along with a splash of the still-hot cooking liquid as needed, and continue whipping energetically until you have a compact but creamy mousse-like consistency, with some larger pieces here and there.

You may need a little more olive oil, or you may find you don't need all of it, and of course the cooking water will help too if the mixture is too dry or too dense (in some parts of the Veneto a splash of milk might be added). This all depends on the texture and quality of the stockfish and how long it was soaked for prior to cooking.

Stockfish (as opposed to salted baccalà) is surprisingly delicate. Season to taste with salt and white pepper and let it cool to room temperature, then serve on thick slices of baguette or grilled white polenta, or try it as a stuffing for fried zucchini (courgette) flowers (see page 125).

How not to stir polenta

IF THE IDEA OF MAKING POLENTA standing at the stove is scaring you off doing it, don't worry. There is instant polenta, of course, but if you'd rather not go there (I wouldn't), there are some shortcuts. Contrary to popular belief, you do not need to stir the entire cooking time. The thick coating that forms on the bottom of the pot as you're stirring will protect the rest of the polenta and keep it smooth, which means you can actually walk away from the stove a little bit here and there and come back and everything will be just as you left it.

In her *Classic Food of Northern Italy*, Milan-born Anna Del Conte, who is considered the doyenne of Italian food writing (and is, at the time of writing, ninety-six years of age!) dares to suggest that cooking polenta from cold water instead of the usual boiling water method is much easier – there is 'no risk of lumps, and the final result is just as good'. She points out that it is only because of tradition that Italians still cook polenta by adding the cornmeal

to boiling water. 'In country kitchens of the sixteenth century, the water was always boiling in the *paiolo* (copper pot) hanging over the open fire, ready for the cornmeal to be added. When the open fire was replaced by gas or electricity, the ritual was too deeply ingrained for anyone to dream of suggesting there might be an easier way.' It is a revolutionary thought and so, with that blessing, I would like to recommend some unorthodox tips on cooking polenta.

Maria Speck in *Simply Ancient Grains* (2016) has an excellent shortcut where you soak dry polenta in boiling water. Cover completely with plastic wrap (make sure it is touching the surface of the polenta so a skin doesn't form) and leave for at least 8–12 hours (even up to 2 days in the fridge). Then, when ready to cook, add water to loosen, bring it to a simmer and cook while stirring for just 10–12 minutes and it's ready. Anna Del Conte likes to make her polenta in a pressure cooker, which only takes 20 minutes, but she has another low-maintenance technique that she calls *polenta senza bastone* (polenta without the wooden stick). After an initial 5 minutes of stirring the polenta on the stovetop, she transfers it to a buttered overproof dish and bakes it, covered with buttered foil, for 1 hour. While the top retains a crust (much like the protective crust that forms around the pot during regular stovetop cooking), it protects the soft polenta underneath.

Polenta, two ways

Polenta in due modi

USE THIS RECIPE FOR either a pillowy, creamy bed of polenta or – ideal if you have leftover polenta – crostini, which are perfect for grilling or frying and using in place of bread for *cicchetti*. Creamy white polenta is often preferred with seafood but isn't the rule. You might also find polenta not made with the usual cornmeal at all, but with buckwheat, or *grano saraceno* (literally 'Arabic grain'). Some modern *cicchetti* that I've had at Bancogiro, where you can sit on the Grand Canal right near the Rialto, include crostini made with *polenta nera*, where the polenta is tinted dramatically with squid ink. If eating creamy polenta on its own, it is often enriched with butter and cheese too (as the characters Rosaura and Arlecchino in Goldoni's play do: see page 53); however, this plain version is more versatile for different dishes and for turning leftovers into crostini. I supply the traditional method for cooking polenta here, but if you are interested in learning about some revolutionary shortcuts, see 'How not to stir polenta', page 49.

NOTE On the serving sizes. Polenta is quite filling, and although some people manage to eat quite a lot of it, I think portion size here is quite a personal (and cultural) thing, much like other staple starchy comfort foods such as bread, rice and potatoes (I seem to have a bottomless pit for a stomach when it comes to potatoes). I had to laugh when I was researching recipes and I noticed that many Italian recipes will tell you that the measurements opposite will serve two people. I honestly think this would be difficult for four people to get through if this is all they were eating. Anna Del Conte more sensibly suggests 250 g (9 oz) uncooked polenta will serve six, and I thoroughly agree. If you are planning on serving polenta as a smaller plate as *cicchetti*, I think you would even be able to stretch that to 10–12, more in line with the portions this makes of crostini. The size for crostini simply differs depending on how small or large you would like to cut it. It will make twelve good-sized crostini, the size that I think of as ideal for a plate of a few *cicchetti*. But if you want to make them smaller, say, to go with many more *cicchetti*, then you can cut each crostino in half, making twenty-four with this recipe.

*Makes 6–12 serves of soft polenta, or
12–24 crostini*

1 teaspoon salt
250 g (9 oz/1½ cups) polenta (cornmeal,
preferably fine-ground 'fioretto'
polenta)

Place 1 litre (34 fl oz/4 cups) water and the salt in a heavy bottomed pot. Pour the polenta *a pioggia*, 'like rain', into the pot, and bring to a simmer (I know this is unusual; most recipes call for adding polenta to boiling water and whisking briskly to avoid lumps, but read the 'How not to stir polenta' section on page 49).

Keep the heat on low to avoid big bubbles of polenta splashing on you, and stir regularly – not vigorously; you can do it slowly and you can walk away here and there as you do something else in the kitchen – with a wooden spoon for 35–40 minutes. It should develop a protective 'skin' on the bottom of the pot, and it will start pulling away from the sides as it cooks. Taste it – it should feel creamy in your mouth with no bite or graininess.

If you are making a soft and creamy polenta, especially with white polenta, you want to keep the consistency in check by adding 250–500 ml (8½–17 fl oz/1–2 cups) hot water, or more if it is to your liking, to the polenta as you are stirring. You are looking for a smooth, velvety mixture rather like very creamy mashed potatoes. When ready, tip the polenta directly onto serving plates or one large platter if sharing.

If making crostini, you do not need the extra water, but watch the stirring as the polenta should get quite thick by the time the 40 minutes is up, and it might be more tiresome to stir (employ someone to take turns with you if you can).

Tip the polenta onto a wooden board or a greased baking tray. You can use whatever size you have but, for an idea, I like to shape the polenta roughly into a rectangle about 20 × 31 cm (8 × 12 in) (wet hands help make a nice smooth top). When completely cool, use a large, sharp knife to cut into crostini – these could be any size you like. I like a more generous-sized crostino, about 5 × 10 cm (2 × 4 in) to give twelve crostini but, if wanting smaller bites, you could cut these in half to have twenty-four squares roughly 5 × 5 cm (2 × 2 in). Grill on a griddle pan on both sides until the surface is crisp and you can see some browned grill marks, about 5 minutes over a medium–high heat, then top as you wish.

Goldoni's Venice

IT'S HARD TO READ ABOUT Venetian cuisine without being interrupted by some scene from one of Carlo Goldoni's (1707–1793) witty theatrical comedies, which often revolve around the world of the common Venetians, rather than the aristocrats. Because his works are a mirror of popular Venetian culture in the eighteenth century, food is naturally a part of that and, in particular, it's home cooking and the rustic cuisine of trattorie that enter into his theatre. One of his characters is a *fritole*-maker (see page 202), who fries sweet treats on the street, in *Il Mercato di Malmantile* ('The Malmantile Market', 1757); you hear the cries of the marketplace with offerings from the mainland, 'Who wants cockerel, who wants hens, who wants to buy fresh ricotta? Who wants eggs? Pull over here!' And in *Le Donne di Casa Soa* (the title basically translates to 'The Housewives', 1755), written in Venetian, a son is sent to buy sardines from the market to put *in saor* (see page 58). There is also talk of poultry of all kinds, from turkey to pigeon to quail, beef tongue, rice and bread, chocolate, tea and coffee. But probably the most famous passage about food written by Goldoni, and one of the few where a recipe is described in full is, lovingly, about polenta.

In *Donna di Garbo* ('The Fashionable Woman', written in 1743), Rosaura, the young, humble protagonist (revolutionary for starters that Goldoni centres his play around a commoner, but also a woman), describes making polenta to Arlecchino, from lighting the fire to filling up the pot with water to put above the flames. Once the water begins to 'murmur', she'll take 'that ingredient, in powder as beautiful as gold' and, little by little, it will sink into the pot. She goes on to recount how they'll take a spoon each when it's done, and put the polenta onto plates where they'll throw on some butter and grated cheese and they'll eat like emperors, 'And then? And then I'll prepare a couple of carafes of sweet, precious wine, and we'll both enjoy it until it's all finished. What do you think, Arlecchino, will that be okay?'

Senti: aspetteremo che tutti sieno a letto, ed anche quel furbo di Brighella, ch'io non posso vedere; poi pian piano tutti due ce ne anderemo in cucina. Io già avrò preparato il bisogno; onde bel bello accenderemo il fuoco, empiremo una bellissima caldaia d'acqua, e la porremo sopra le fiamme. Quando l'acqua comincierà a mormorare, io prenderò di quell'ingrediente, in polvere bellissima come l'oro, chiamata farina gialla; e a poco a poco anderò fondendola nella caldaia, nella quale tu con una sapientissima verga andrai facendo dei circoli e delle linee. Quando la materia sarà condensata, la leveremo dal fuoco, e tutti due di concerto, con un cucchiaio per uno, la faremo passare dalla caldaia ad un piatto. Vi cacceremo poi sopra di mano in mano un'abbondante porzione di fresco, giallo e delicato butirro, poi altrettanto grasso, giallo e ben grattato formaggio: e poi? E poi Arlecchino e Rosaura, uno da una parte, l'altro dall'altra, con una forcina in mano per cadauno, prenderemo due o tre bocconi in una volta di quella ben condizionata polenta e ne faremo una mangiata da imperadore; e poi? E poi preparerò un paio di fiaschi di dolcissimo, preziosissimo vino, e tutti due ce li goderemo sino all'intiera consumazione. Che ti pare, Arlecchino, anderà bene così?

The arrival of maize: the so-called 'Turkish' grain

ONE OF THE MOST IMPORTANT elements of Venetian cooking is the humble accompaniment to so many – if not all – dishes: polenta. It is, as Anna Del Conte says in *The Classic Food of Northern Italy*, 'a golden thread running through the cooking of northern Italy', but this staple is most popular in the Veneto, which is where it first arrived from Mexico via a brief stop in Seville – and where the first bag of maize was sold at the Rialto market in 1495.

By 1540, it was planted as an ornamental plant and cultivated in the area. There is a stunning frescoed ceiling in Palazzo Grimani – a gem of a museum in the heart of Venice – where, among the water birds and native grapes, figs, olives and oleander, you can find possibly the earliest depiction of corn in Italy, painted around 1563 by Camillo Mantovano (see page 52). The Grimani, who counted Doges and Cardinals among their family members, owned significant land in the Venetian countryside of Polesine. This strip of land between the Po and Adige rivers that today would be in the province of Rovigo was abundant in corn fields – probably the exact ones described by the Venetian geographer Giovanni Battista Ramusio in his *Delle Navigationi et Viaggi* (1554): 'The admirable and famous sowing of maize of the western Indies, of which there have already arrived in Italy in colours of white and red, and above the Polesine of Rhoigo [Rovigo] and Villa bona [Villa d'Adige] are planted whole fields of both colours.' There was an economic crisis after the discovery of the Americas, and Venice found itself with a little less traffic, so they could appreciate how useful cornmeal was at keeping hunger at bay.

Although native to the Americas, the first sack of maize arriving after a long voyage from a distant land was assumed to have come from Turkey ('As most good things brought to Venice by sea came from Turkey', along with other treasures, from gold to carpets and perfumes). So to this day it is still called *granoturco*, Turkish grain, Ada Boni points out in *Italian Regional Cooking*.

Polenta is used as a filling, soft and creamy porridge of sorts, often enriched with butter and cheese (as it is in Gaetano Zompini's etching of the Venetian polenta street seller in his series *Le Arti che Vanno per Via Nella Città di Venezia*), or supporting a rich and full-flavoured meat or fish dish. It can be left to set and then cut into slices and grilled or fried in both savoury and sweet treats. It can be made into gnocchi and is also used in sweet puddings, cakes and biscuits. As Gillian Riley notes in *The Oxford Companion to Italian Food*, 'Polenta is comfort food combined with visual pleasure', and this brings to mind Pietro Longhi's eighteenth-century oil painting *La Polenta*, which is in Venice's Ca' Rezzonico. Two men are seated at a table, while the focus is on two voluptuous, red-faced (presumably from standing over the fire for the good part of an hour) women, one holding the *bastone*, or long wooden stick used for stirring polenta, the other pouring the polenta out of the *paiolo* (copper pot) directly onto the white tablecloth. One of the men is staring adoringly at the polenta.

In Venice, also popular is a delicate white polenta. A white variety of corn known as *biancoperla*, with aptly named pearly white kernels on long, elegant tapered cobs, is grown exclusively in eastern Veneto between Treviso, Venice, Padova and Rovigo by relatively few producers, and is today a Slow Food presidium – in other words, it is considered a native product with important cultural significance worth protecting. Even in the sixteenth century there were accounts of white corn grown in the region, and it was already considered prestigious, reserved for nobility. It had its peak in the nineteenth century but, according to the Slow Food Foundation, after the Second World War a decline in popularity began as higher-yielding hybrid corn varieties from America took the place of *biancoperla* in the fields until it was almost extinct. It is usually made as a very, very soft polenta, served in a perfectly creamy white puddle often paired with seafood such as fried *moeche* (soft-shell crabs), grilled prawns (shrimp) or fried *schie*, tiny Venetian grey prawns that are eaten whole.

Vicenza-style baccalà

Baccalà alla Vicentina

THIS DISH, AS YOU MAY be able to tell from its name, comes from the neighbouring city of Vicenza (which became part of La Serenissima in the fifteenth century), about 80 km (50 miles) west of the Venetian lagoon. This careful preparation with a list of punchy ingredients is often displayed in Venetian _bàcari_ next to the understated, elegant _baccalà mantecato_ and I have to admit I cannot resist either and usually order both _cicchetti_. It is such a revered dish (Ada Boni calls it 'one of the finest of all Venetian dishes') that there is a confraternity dedicated to it that dates to 1987 and, naturally, a codified recipe – this one that I recount opposite – to ensure that the 400-year-old tradition is respected. Saying that, there is an interesting recipe in gastronomes Luigi Carnacina and Luigi Veronelli's _Cucina Rustica Regionale_ from 1974 for _Baccalà alla Vicentina_, which includes the additions of cinnamon, garlic and white wine – and the whole thing is cooked in double the quantity of milk called for in the codified recipe by the _Venerabile Confraternità del Bacalà alla Vicentina_ (yes, the one 'c' is intentional, as it is the dialect spelling).

This is typically made with the revived cod pieces tightly and neatly packed into a terracotta dish placed over a low fire – imagine in the low and slow-dying heat of a wood-fired cooking range – for 4½ hours. But I find in a modern kitchen this length of cooking is difficult to maintain without drying out the ingredients (according to an old saying, _baccalà_ is one of the three foods that gets harder as it cooks, along with liver

and eggs). If you don't have a terracotta pot for cooking in, which gives a very unique flavour to the whole dish, try this in a cast-iron casserole dish or something with a heavy bottom and a tight-fitting lid. I very much like leftovers the next day when the flavours have developed – you can add a splash of milk or water to warm it up; it is at its best warm.

Cinnamon and Salt

Serves 6–8

500 g (1 lb 2 oz) pre-soaked baccalà
  (unsalted dried stockfish; see Note
  on page 46)
2 tablespoons plain (all-purpose) flour
2–3 salted preserved anchovies or
  sardines, or anchovies preserved in oil
250 ml (8½ fl oz/1 cup) extra-virgin olive oil
1 white onion, sliced
a few parsley sprigs, finely chopped
250 ml (8½ fl oz/1 cup) full-cream
  (whole) milk
2 tablespoons grated parmesan
polenta crostini or soft polenta, to serve

NOTE Salted sardines are used in the original recipe, but if you have trouble getting these, salted anchovies are similar – these are both fleshier than the more common preserved anchovies in oil and require a tiny bit more effort to prepare for cooking. First, you need to rinse off the excess salt then soak for 15 minutes in fresh water. Open the fish in half lengthways, starting from the tail end, and remove the spine as you go. If you cannot get stockfish for this recipe, you can try this with salted cod, but be aware it is a drastic change to the codified recipe! It will work though, and it is still delicious. You will have a meatier consistency and the oil may not absorb as much as it seems to do with stockfish, so you may not need as much.

Remove the skin and bones of the stockfish and cut into pieces. If you have difficulty doing this, I find poaching the fish for 2–3 minutes in water makes it much easier. Dust the pieces in the flour.

Prepare the anchovies (or sardines) as described in the note, then chop finely. With about 60 ml (2 fl oz/¼ cup) of the olive oil, gently cook the onion over a low heat in a terracotta or heavy bottomed (such as cast iron) casserole dish until softened, about 5 minutes. Add the prepared sardines, stir through and continue cooking for a further minute, then sprinkle over the parsley.

Add the pieces of floured cod, distributing evenly among the onion mixture, and cover with the rest of the ingredients, including a good pinch of salt and some freshly ground pepper. The fish should be submerged in liquid; if not, top up with a little milk. Cook, covered, on the lowest heat possible, barely simmering, until the milk is absorbed and the fish is softer and flaking, about 1½ hours. You aren't supposed to stir this dish at all according to the codified recipe, but do check every now and then that the heat isn't too high and nothing is sticking on the bottom. Transfer to a nice bowl and break up the larger pieces of fish, scooping out the creamy onion mixture from the saucepan. Serve on slices of grilled yellow polenta crostini as *cicchetti*, or over soft polenta as a warming, hearty meal – this dish is not usually served with sides.

Sweet-and-sour fried sardines

Sarde in saor

MY FAVOURITE OF ALL of Venice's *cicchetti* is also among the most classic on offer at any *bàcaro* and is one of the traditional dishes that Venetians take on their boats with them, along with *Bovoletti* (see page 74) and roast duck for the Festa del Redentore, a joyful festival held on the third Sunday of July that celebrates the end of the Plague of 1576.

Preparing food *in saor*, the technique of marinating fried food in vinegar and other ingredients, was a favourite Venetian way of conserving food for long trips (Venetian gastronome and actor Giuseppe Maffioli called it *cibo dei marinai*, sailor's food) and it can be likened to Portuguese escabeche and Japanese *nanbanzuke*. Although sardines are Venice's most popular ingredient to prepare *in saor,* you can also find it with scampi, sole, plump prawns (shrimp), freshwater fish such as carp and trout, chicken, or vegetables such as radicchio (see page 100). Because it is a dish that lends itself well to being prepared in advance, *in saor* is a preparation that Ines de Benedetti in her Italian Jewish cookbook *Poesia Nascosta: Le ricette della cucina tradizionale ebraica italiana* (2013) writes 'was never missing on Saturdays in the homes of good Jews'. Venice's Jewish quarter is where you can find fried eggplant (aubergine) or pumpkin *in saor*, with finely chopped mint.

The recipe for *sarde in saor* can be traced to the 1300s in one of Italy's earliest-known cookbooks, the *Libro per Cuoco* by the so-called *anonimo veneziano*, the 'anonymous Venetian'. It calls for sliced white onions cooked in oil and vinegar topping fried sardines, kept in a terracotta dish. Although the recipe hasn't changed much since then, there are always variations based on personal preferences and family traditions. My friend Valeria Necchio makes hers without 'much adornment', as she says in her cookbook, *Veneto*, but with a touch of sugar together with the vinegar. Another friend of mine makes it with slices of lemon instead of vinegar and without the raisins or pine nuts. At the well-known *bàcaro* Al Mascaron, the dish has the addition of fresh bay leaves, coriander seeds and white, pink and black pepper – and they do a version with veal liver too, which has a touch of fresh ginger in it. In Mariù Salvatori de Zuliani's classic Venetian cookbook *A Tola Co I Nostri Veci*, she supplies two recipes, one with a marinade of onions, vinegar and sugar, the other with the addition of sultanas, pine nuts and cinnamon. She notes that sultanas and pine nuts are usually added in the winter, while the summer version doesn't need them. And sometimes – for those who truly love the sweet part of sweet-and-sour – you'll even find it with the addition of candied citron.

Serves 4 as a light lunch, or makes 12 cicchetti

12 fresh sardines, cleaned, heads and
    backbones removed, butterflied
1½ tablespoons plain (all-purpose) flour,
    or enough for dusting
vegetable oil, for frying
40 g (1½ oz/⅓ cup) raisins
60 ml (2 fl oz/¼ cup) white wine,
    or water
1 large white onion, peeled and
    thinly sliced
2 tablespoons extra-virgin olive oil
125 ml (4 fl oz/1/2 cup) white-wine vinegar
pinch of ground cloves (optional)
1 teaspoon whole coriander seeds,
    crushed (optional)
pinch of sugar (optional)
1½ tablespoons pine nuts
fresh or toasted sliced baguette or
    grilled polenta, to serve

Dust the sardine fillets in the flour and shallow-fry in oil for 1 minute each side over a medium–high heat until golden and crisp. Season with salt and set aside on some kitchen paper to drain until needed.

Soak the raisins in the white wine for 15 minutes to soften them. Meanwhile, cook the onion gently in a frying pan with the olive oil just until it is soft and transparent, about 10 minutes on a low heat, then add the vinegar, the wine from the raisins (set the raisins aside), some freshly ground pepper and the spices, if using. Let it simmer gently for about 10 minutes, then remove from the heat. Taste the mixture; if it is too sharp, stir in a pinch of sugar.

In a small terrine or deep dish, place a layer of sardines, top them with some of the onions, some of the raisins and the pine nuts, and continue layering until the sardines are used up, then top with a layer of onions, raisins and pine nuts, and finish with the rest of the vinegar sauce poured over the top. Cover and allow to marinate for at least 24 hours in the fridge before serving. This keeps well in the fridge for up to 1 week.

These are best eaten at room temperature, removing from the fridge an hour before you want to enjoy them. Serve the sardines on slices of toasted or fresh baguette, or grilled polenta.

Sweet-and-sour radicchio

Radicchio in saor

THIS IS A WONDERFUL VEGETARIAN
version of *Sarde in saor* (opposite) using
one of the Veneto's best vegetables –
radicchio. There are several types, but
I like the mildly bitter Treviso variety
(from the eponymous town north of
Venice) for this recipe with its long,
oblong shape in the early-harvest
version. There is also the elegant
late-harvest Treviso, which has long,
curled, tentacle-like leaves and makes
a striking looking dish, but if you can
only get Chioggia, the round one from
just south of Venice, it will work fine
too. Like all *in saor* preparation, this is
best done the day before to allow the
flavours to mingle.

Makes 8 cicchetti

1 white onion, thinly sliced
60 ml (2 fl oz/¼ cup) olive oil
125 ml (4 fl oz/½ cup) white wine
2 radicchio di Treviso heads, quartered
 lengthways
60 ml (2 fl oz/¼ cup) white-wine vinegar
1 heaped tablespoon raisins, soaked in
 white wine or water

In a wide, shallow frying pan, cook the
onion gently in the olive oil over a low–
medium heat with a pinch of salt, about
5 minutes. Initially, you want to keep the
onion soft and pale, almost transparent.
As soon as there is any danger of
colouring, douse the pan with white wine,
then you can turn the heat up and let the
wine bubble furiously for a few minutes.

Add the radicchio, followed by the
vinegar and the raisins in their wine or
water. Turn the heat to low and let it
simmer, stirring and turning occasionally
to keep the radicchio semi-submerged,
until tender, about 10 minutes, depending
on how large or tough the leaves are.
Remove from the heat, let cool and then
place in an airtight container in the fridge
overnight to marinate. Serve at room
temperature the next day.

Fondi di articiocchi

YOU WILL COME ACROSS these in the Rialto market: perfectly trimmed, round, pale grey-green discs swimming in a bucket of water, ready to take home and be cooked with garlic and stock and eaten with a glass of wine. Or you might be lost, wandering the dark alleyways near the market and come across open doors revealing someone peeling crates and crates of artichokes directly onto the terrazzo floor, more or less just as humanist and long-time Venetian resident Giacomo Castelvetro (1546–1616) described in his letters. Or perhaps you've stumbled into a classic *bàcaro* like Do Mori with its dark wood interior, copper pots on the ceiling and old-school *cicchetti* on display and there'll be a plate of these humble-looking medallions of artichoke bottoms with a toothpick through them and you'll know you could only be in Venice.

Makes 6 cicchetti

6 globe artichokes
1 lemon, halved
60 ml (2 fl oz/¼ cup) olive oil
1 garlic clove
60 ml (2 fl oz/¼ cup) vegetable stock,
    or white wine
white pepper, to taste
a few parsley sprigs, finely chopped

Prepare a bowl of cold water, squeeze half a lemon into it and then leave the lemon in the water.

Peel off the outer leaves of the artichoke until they become pale and very tender. Holding the stem, cut the artichoke about 1 cm (½ in) from the base. Rub the cut part of the base with the other lemon half to prevent it from oxidising. Trim the base of any green parts or extra little leaves and scoop out the fluffy choke with a teaspoon. Place the artichoke bottom into the bowl of lemon water and continue with the rest of the artichokes.

Pour the olive oil into a saucepan and, over a low–medium heat, add the whole garlic clove and let it infuse the oil gently for a minute or so without letting it brown. Add the artichokes to the garlic oil and let them sizzle a moment, then follow with the stock. Add a pinch of salt and some white pepper and let it simmer for 15–20 minutes, or until the artichoke bottoms are very tender. Garnish with parsley and some of the cooking liquid.

Castraure, lagoon artichokes from the island of Sant'-Erasmo

VENICE'S HIGHLY PRIZED *castraure* are nothing more than the first new baby artichokes of the Violetto variety (named for its violet colour), pruned or 'castrated' (as their name might tell you) from the top of the plant in April so that the rest of the plant will efficiently grow more and larger artichokes (known as *botoli*) later in the season, which continues until June. These little gems, so sweet and tender, are eaten simply – raw, with the leaves dipped in olive oil seasoned with salt and pepper, akin to Tuscany's *pinzimonio*, sliced thinly in salad or deep-fried in batter, for example. You can more easily find the larger *botoli*, which might be served as *cicchetti*, simply boiled and served with olive oil, salt and pepper, at their simplest, or with the addition of garlic, parsley and vinegar.

They are mostly grown on the island of Sant'Erasmo, the largest in the lagoon after Venice itself. It has long been known as Venice's 'vegetable patch'; even Francesco Sansovino in his *Venetia, Citta Nobilissima et Singolare*, written in 1581, describes it as full of gardens and vineyards, abundant in herbs and fruit. You can find a handful of producers scattered around the lagoon's islands, including Mazzorbo, Vignole and Lio Piccolo, too. It is the sandy, saline soil that gets credit for creating such exquisitely sweet and uniquely Venetian produce – once it was fertilised with *scoasse*, the Venetian word for rubbish, or 'crab and other shell debris', writes Gillian Riley in *The Oxford Companion of Italian Food*, to contrast the acidity in the soil. But the other thing that makes these *castraure* so rare and sought after is their availability – 10, maybe 15 days of harvest and that's it.

Grilled scampi

Scampi grigliati

SIMPLY GRILLED SHELLFISH is a classic of Venetian cuisine and you could do this preparation with any large prawns (shrimp) or live *canocchie* (mantis shrimp) or other shellfish, such as long *cappelunghe* (razor clams), and serve it the same way with this classic Venetian finish of olive oil and finely minced garlic and parsley, the '*ancestrale salsina*' or 'ancestral sauce', as Giuseppe Maffioli called it. There is something about scampi in Venice for me, straight from the fishmongers at the Rialto where they are so fresh and sweet you could simply eat them raw. There is not much else you need to do to them except ensure you have a good pot of polenta ready at hand.

Serves 4

1 garlic clove, finely chopped
a few parsley sprigs, finely chopped
2–3 tablespoons extra-virgin olive oil
4 fresh, whole scampi
polenta or crostini, to serve

Combine the garlic, parsley and olive oil in a small bowl and set aside.

With a sharp, heavy knife, cut the whole scampi lengthways directly down the middle to split them in half.

Get a griddle pan ready over a high heat. When it is very hot, place the scampi, cut-side down first, and sear, turning once, for a total of no more than 60 seconds.

Place on a plate and immediately scatter over the herby, garlicky olive oil. Serve with warm, creamy polenta (see page 50), or crostini.

NOTE I also love serving these scampi on a platter together with about a dozen razor clams, which are known as *cappelunghe* in Venetian dialect and are found readily in the Rialto market when in season. You will need to purge the razor clams and clean them of their sand. Sandro Brandolisio in his book on *cicchetti* in the 1950s and 60s describes going down the canal to get a bucket of water to purge the *cappelunghe* in – today, you would be better off using tap water with sea salt added to it. I go with 35 g (1¼ oz) salt per litre (34 fl oz/4 cups) water, which is the same salinity as seawater. Place the shells in a wide, shallow dish, such as a baking dish, so they don't have to go to much effort to open up, and cover with the water. Leave them to purge for an hour or so. Rinse them well in fresh water and they are ready to be steamed open with half a glass of wine in a very hot pan and served the same way as the scampi. I like to serve scampi and any shellfish with all their shells on. Halving the scampi helps you eat them with your hands, plucking out the prized meat. But, if you prefer, you can remove the shells before serving. It's nowhere near as fun to eat or as pretty to look at though.

Baby octopus with celery

Moscardini col sedano

THIS IS A BRIGHT AND REFRESHING dish, with a delightful crunch of celery that I just adore with tender octopus. You could add boiled potatoes to this, or halved fresh cherry tomatoes or marinated black olives. But I do enjoy the simplicity of this two-ingredient salad. In journalist Sandro Brandolisio's charming book, *Cichéti* (2019), which recounts the typical *cicchetti* found in Venice's *bàcari* in the 1950s and 60s, the recipes, written in Italian, Venetian dialect and English, are just a paragraph each and don't have measurements but are a description of how to prepare the traditional *cicchetti* from this period. This is how I have interpreted his *Folpeti col sèano*.

NOTE The octopus needs to be cleaned before using. If bought frozen, they usually have already been cleaned. If fresh, you can ask your fishmonger to do this or, to do it at home, simply remove the beak, cut out the eyes, empty the head and rinse thoroughly.

Makes 6 cicchetti

3 medium-sized baby octopus (about 500 g/1 lb 2 oz)
2 celery stalks, leaves and all, finely sliced
2 tablespoons olive oil
juice of ½ lemon
grilled polenta, to serve

Bring a pot of water (deep enough to cover the octopus) to a rolling boil. Some like to make the tentacles extra curly; to do this, dip the octopus in the boiling water up to its tentacles, then pull it out and repeat two or three times until the tentacles are curled. Immerse them in the boiling water, turn the heat down to a simmer over a low–medium heat and cook until they are very tender (a fork should easily pierce through), about 45 minutes. Remove from the water and, when cool enough to handle, pull the skin off (which can be a little gelatinous). Rinse, then roughly chop each octopus, separating the tentacles.

Place in a bowl. Add the celery and its leaves with the olive oil, lemon juice and salt and pepper, adjusting the seasoning to your taste, then toss together. Serve with grilled polenta.

Classici

Octopus in wine

Polpi in tecia

I LOVE THIS SIMPLE PREPARATION
for octopus cooked in red wine, inspired
by a recipe from Mariù Salvadori de
Zuliani's book, *A Tola Co I Nostri Veci*,
which translates to 'At the table with
our elders'. It reminds me of a recipe
that Sandro Brandolisio describes in his
book on *cicchetti* in the 1950s and 60s
for *polipetti* or *moscardini* (as these small
octopus are known in Venice) *a scotta
dito*, which means 'burn your fingers'.
A large, piping-hot pot of *moscardini*
would be placed directly on the counter,
and they were eaten right out of the pot
without any condiments, washed down
with a glass of wine to 'put out the fire
in your throat'.

You can serve these on slices of grilled
polenta crostini (see page 50), or just
on their own with a toothpick.

Makes approx. 12 cicchetti

60 ml (2 fl oz/¼ cup) olive oil
500 g (1 lb 2 oz) baby octopus (about 12)
500 ml (17 fl oz/2 cups) red wine
pinch of ground cloves
1 bay leaf
1 garlic clove

Heat the olive oil in a saucepan. Sear the
octopus all over and, when they turn
bright pink, about 2 minutes, pour over
the red wine, adding enough water to
cover the octopus. Add the cloves, bay
leaf and garlic, then cover with a lid and
simmer over a gentle heat until tender,
about 45–60 minutes.

Stewed cuttlefish with peas

Seppie con piselli

THIS IS AN ABSOLUTELY DELICIOUS combination of two favourite Venetian ingredients: cuttlefish and peas. I first ate this *'seppie in tecia'* on the island of Torcello while visiting friends Edoardo and Krystina. They took us to a cheerful self-service trattoria aptly called Taverna Tipica Veneziana set in a huge garden and, with all our children running around, we had this cuttlefish, along with sweet prawns (shrimp) *in saor*, fried calamari and plenty of cold drinks. It was all just perfect.

Serves 6 as cicchetti, or 2 as a main

400 g (14 oz) whole baby cuttlefish
60 ml (2 fl oz/¼ cup) olive oil
½ onion, sliced thinly
60 ml (2 fl oz/¼ cup) white wine
125 ml (4 fl oz/½ cup) tomato passata
 (puréed tomatoes)
1 garlic clove, finely chopped
1 slice prosciutto, finely chopped
100 g (3½ oz) fresh or snap-frozen peas
handful of parsley, very finely chopped

See note for preparing the cuttlefish.

In a wide pan or casserole dish, heat half the olive oil and gently cook the onion with a pinch of salt over a low heat for about 5 minutes, or until it begins to soften but not colour. Add the cuttlefish and continue cooking for 1 minute, then pour over the wine. Turn the heat up to medium and let the wine simmer and reduce for a few minutes, then add the tomato and about 250 ml (8½ fl oz/1 cup) water, or to cover, salt and freshly ground pepper, and simmer, uncovered, until the cuttlefish is very tender, about 35 minutes depending on how large the cuttlefish are.

Meanwhile, in a separate wide, shallow pan, heat the rest of the olive oil, add the garlic and prosciutto and sizzle gently over a low heat for a minute or so, then add the peas along with about 250 ml (8½ fl oz/1 cup) water and turn up to medium heat. Let simmer, uncovered, for about 5 minutes, or until the peas are tender but still bright green. Set aside until the cuttlefish is ready, then unite the cuttlefish and the peas in one pan and cook for a minute or two so that they get to know each other. Scatter over the parsley.

NOTE If the cuttlefish are really small, leave them whole, but they should be cleaned if they aren't already. It sounds gruesome, but it is quite quick and easy. First, locate the beak (in the middle of the tentacles) and just pull it out. Cut out the eyes and pull out the innards and small bone from the body (including carefully removing the ink sac), and pull off the skin, which is like a very thin membrane and easy to do while you pull the wings off. You should be left with just the white flesh, mostly intact. If the cuttlefish are frozen, they are often already cleaned, or ask your fishmonger to do this for you. If you buy them larger, then you can clean them as described and slice into strips. The tentacles can be left in a tuft or, if they are rather long or large, cut them lengthways and/or in half. You can also use calamari for this, which are longer in shape and generally have thinner flesh than rounder squid.

If eating as a main, serve with polenta. Leftovers are absolutely delicious, even tossed through pasta or piled onto crostini, and the whole baby cuttlefish, served cold, make very nice *cicchetti* just on the end of a toothpick.

Bovoletti

YOU'LL SEE THESE TINY SNAILS with their brown- and white-spiralled shells, also called *bovoeti*, in big trays at the Rialto market, where they're very much live and active. They're land snails, but they're found near the sea and make up a favourite Venetian dish – one you'll find Venetians feasting on at Christmas Eve or for the summer festival of the Redentore, on long tables lining the esplanade of the Giudecca, or in their boats while watching fireworks, along with *sarde in saor*, stuffed duck and plenty of wine.

Watching the *bovoletti* crawl over each other at the market one day while in line for the fishmonger, the elderly woman in front of me ordered a kilo of them. '*Mi scusi*', I asked her, how do you prepare them? And she proceeded to tell me the recipe. First, place them in a pot of lightly salted water for a couple of hours (oh, and cover it because otherwise they'll escape). Drain, then wash them under running water and refill the pot with fresh water, then place over a low heat. When you see the snails have come out of their shells (again, the lid is handy so they don't escape), add salt, turn up the heat and simmer rapidly for 2 minutes and they're ready. Drain and dress the snails with abundant finely chopped garlic and parsley, olive oil, salt and pepper. They're best prepared a couple of hours in advance so they take on the flavours of the dressing. Serve them with toothpicks to pull the snails out of their shells and eat them with polenta.

Ada Boni describes how to purge them in her book *Italian Regional Cooking* as so: leave them for 2 days in a wicker basket with a few vine leaves and some pieces of bread soaked in water, covered to prevent them escaping.

Dressed new potatoes

Patatine condite

SANDRO BRANDOLISIO WRITES THAT potatoes need washing down with wine (see page 38 for more on what makes the ideal *cicchetti*), and that at one point these boiled potatoes with garlic and parsley were found in every *bàcaro* in Venice for this reason – since eating them calls for ordering another round of *ombre*. As a potato-lover, I am delighted that this is the case and that you can still find simply boiled or roasted potatoes, maybe strung together on a skewer, or on their own pierced with a toothpick, around Venice, such as at All'Antica Mola. These, together with the boiled eggs (see opposite), as simple as they may be, are among my favourite *cicchetti* to order.

Serves 6–8 as cicchetti

500 g (1 lb 2 oz) whole new baby potatoes
1 garlic clove
a few parsley sprigs
2 tablespoons olive oil

Give the potatoes a good brush in a bowl of water if they haven't already had a clean, and then place them in a saucepan. Cover with cold water, add a good pinch or two of salt, then bring to the boil and cook until the tip of a knife or a fork tine easily enters the centre of the potato, about 15 minutes. In the meantime, finely chop the garlic and parsley. When the potatoes are cooked, drain them, then, while hot, toss with the garlic, parsley, olive oil and a generous pinch of salt. Serve hot or cold.

Boiled eggs, a few ways

Uova sode in vari modi

WHENEVER I SEE BOILED EGGS IN a counter full of *cicchetti*, whole or halved and served skewered with a silky anchovy draped over them, or with a boiled prawn (shrimp), with crunchy fennel or a pickled onion, or even on their own, I will always order one – or more. Boiled eggs have an important place culturally and historically too, being that they are so wonderfully portable and nutritious. They were particularly useful for travellers in a place like maritime Venice, for pilgrimages, or for those who worked long hours away from home.

Makes 6 cicchetti

3 eggs
2 large prawns (shrimp)
2 anchovies preserved in oil
1 teaspoon mayonnaise
2 thin slices fennel, plus some fronds

Bring a small saucepan filled with at least 3 cm (1¼ in) water to a gentle simmer over a medium heat. Once simmering, lower in the eggs and cover. Cook them for 8 minutes for an ever-so-slightly jammy yolk, or leave them for an extra minute for a harder-set yolk. Remove with a slotted spoon and plunge the eggs into a bowl of cold water. Let them cool for about 10 minutes. If not using right away, you can keep whole boiled eggs at this point in the fridge for up to a week.

To peel the eggs neatly, submerge the hard-boiled eggs in a bowl of water. Tap them gently repeatedly while moving the egg around to crack the shell all over, then start picking it off. While it is underwater, the water will get in through the broken shell and separate the membrane from the whites, which is what will give you a neat boiled egg. Peel off the shell and pat the egg dry, then continue with the rest.

Slice the eggs in half lengthways, place on a serving plate and sprinkle with a pinch of salt.

To prepare the prawns, bring a small saucepan of water to the boil and add the prawns, whole, and poach them for 1 minute. Remove from the water, pat dry and, when cool enough to handle, peel off the shell and tail.

Top two of the egg halves with a prawn each. Top another two of the egg halves with an anchovy fillet each, and top the last two with ½ teaspoon mayonnaise each and a small slice of fennel, decorating with a tuft of some of the green fronds. Secure the toppings to the eggs with toothpicks where needed.

NOTE Older eggs are easier to peel, so if you are hoping to get attractive-looking boiled eggs, buy them a few days before you would like to serve them. The timing of these perfectly hard-boiled eggs takes into account that you are using eggs straight from the fridge. If using room-temperature eggs, you can shave off 1 minute.

Classici

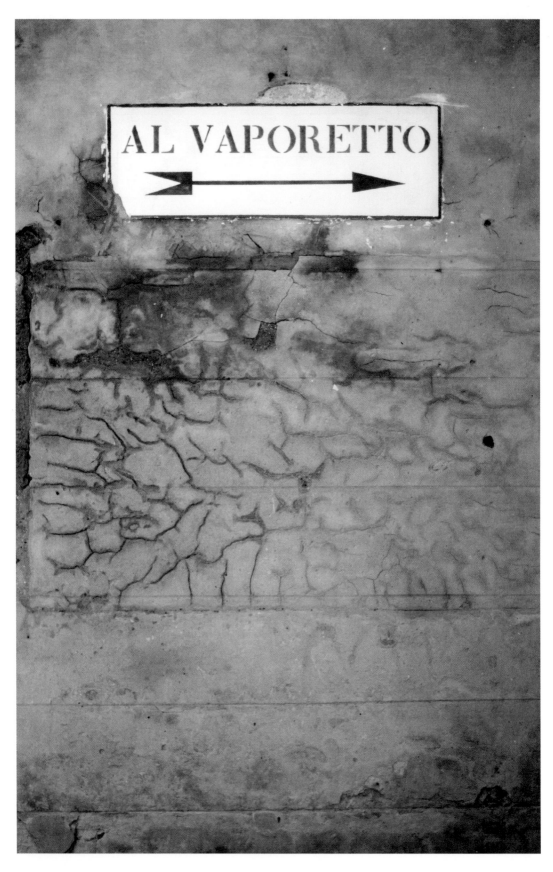

To the vaporetto

Ombre at All'Arco

A canal in the Giudecca

Moderni
Moderni
Moderni
Moderni
Moderni

Moderni Modern cicchetti	*Brioche di tonno affumicato, cren e crema di carciofi* Smoked tuna, horseradish and artichoke buns
	Crema di peperone e melanzane grigliate *per francobolli* Roasted capsicum cream and grilled eggplant for little sandwiches
	Tramezzini di gamberetti e rucola Prawn and rocket sandwiches
	Tramezzini di asparagi e uova Asparagus and egg sandwiches
	Crostini con crema di radicchio e noci Crostini with radicchio and walnut cream
	Crostini con sgombro, olive e pinoli Crostini with mackerel, olives and pine nuts
	Branzino marinato al cumino Cured sea bass with cumin
	Tartare di tonno Tuna tartare
	Mostarda di carote con senape e prosciutto arrosto Carrot mostarda with mustard and roast ham
	Gamberi e lardo Prawns wrapped in lardo

From osteria to bàcaro: places to eat and drink in Venice

The importance of selling wine in Venice can be traced back to one simple need: Venice had everything, but it did not have good drinking water. Water was expensive, wells were few and wine was an affordable way to quench the thirst of even the poorest of Venetians. Wine-selling in Venice was so important that Renaissance wine merchants had their own guild, based in San Silvestro, close to the Rialto.

In the preface of *Osterie a Venezia* (1978), Mario Stefani recounts how water from wells was often contaminated by dead birds, or the presence of sewer rats, cats and dogs, and how severe laws had been made to ensure people didn't purposefully pollute them, such as when the cadaver of a man had been found in the bottom of a well, murdered and disposed of by his wife and her lover.

The relationship between the people of Venice and wine naturally became entangled in the serving of food too. In fact, many Venetian food writers point out that Venetian cuisine – and here I would stress the *way* Venetian food is eaten, in particular – without the company of wine would not make much sense. They go together. The *osteria* in Venice is still synonymous with a kind of bar rather than a restaurant as it is in the rest of Italy – a place for people to gather and socialise over a drink and a nibble, an ever-important reference point for this pedestrian city. In medieval Venice it functioned as a place serving food and drink on the ground floor with rooms for accommodation on the floors above.

In 1347 there were twenty-four *osterie* in Venice, and still just twenty-three in the Renaissance (the numbers were strictly regulated), where they were concentrated around the quarters of San Marco and the Rialto – where you still find the highest concentration of traditional *bàcari*. As the centuries went on, however, the popularity and importance of these social spots was such that it was hard to stop the rise of *osterie* – in the early 1900s you could count, in just San Marco's quarter, one *osteria* for every sixty-nine residents and at Malamocco, on Venice's Lido, there were seventy-four *osterie* for its 900 residents – one for every twelve residents. Today, there are about 120, according to food historian Carla Coco, although they have now become known as *bàcari,* the traditional wine bars that have been 'practising happy hour for centuries', as she says.

There are numerous names for similar places that sold wine to suit all tastes and pockets. Although, of these, just the *bàcari* still exist, what does remain in Venice are the street names indicating a *magazen* or a *malvasia* was nearby.

Caneva, a bottega that sold wine (in Venice, historically, also salt). Its name comes from the Latin for *cantina*, wine cellar.

Furatole, hole-in-the-wall botteghe that sold food such as soups, bread and fried fish, generally for a poorer clientele. They were not allowed to sell wine.

Bàcaro, a name coined by a *gondoliere* when describing '*vino da far baldoria* (*bacara* in dialect)' or wine to make merry with. They've remained essentially like the old *osterie*, not serving a full meal or necessarily having sit-down tables. Frequented by modest clients who perhaps did not have the time (or the economic means) to sit down for a full meal and were satisfied with a bite to eat on the run.

Magazen da vin, a kind of tavern that sold wine to the public (you could even pawn objects to be paid back in cash and wine, usually bad wine), but sometimes also secretly functioned as a brothel with rooms out the back.

Malvasia, named for the Greek grapes that supplied the Venetians with a sweet wine that was particularly appreciated in the lagoon – here, they only sold imported wines and no food. They had their own guild, separate from the regular wine merchant's guild.

Wine from the lagoon

I got up before the sun and, camera in hand, crept down along the eerily quiet canal lined with the low, candy-coloured houses of Burano, a *vaporetto* ride across the lagoon from Venice. It was traditionally an island inhabited by fishermen, so Matteo Bisol, the director of Venissa Tenuta, explained to me as he showed me around the day before, so the buildings are simpler, smaller and more rustic than the elegant *palazzi* in Venice. Indeed, their miniature status makes them all the more charming and 'cute'. I later read the fishermen painted their homes in bright colours so they could spot them from far away – certainly, in the grey fog of the lagoon in autumn and winter, these rainbow houses would stand out.

I crossed the wooden bridge that connects Burano island to the island of Mazzorbo, to head to Venissa, a beautiful resort surrounded on three sides by water with a Michelin-starred restaurant, rooms above and the walls of an abandoned monastery enclosing a passionate project – to revive a native Venetian grape. I found the garden gate open, and went in to find a team of harvesters already at work picking grapes as the sun began to rise.

In 2002, Matteo Bisol's father, Gianluca Bisol – a Prosecco producer whose family have been winemakers in the Valdobbiadene since 1542 – came across an unusual white grape in a garden on the island of Torcello. It turned out to be the Dorona, an ancient variety native to Venice that was thought to have been wiped out by the 1966 flood. Bisol and his family now cultivate a hectare of Dorona vines inside the Tenuta's ancient wall, overlooked by the crooked fourteenth-century bell tower. The garden is shared with a vegetable patch and fruit trees that cover another hectare, and are tended to by pensioners from Burano.

The wine made from these grapes is a complex, amber-toned white wine, which is macerated with skins on for 40 days so it has the body and structure of a red – an age-old, traditional treatment of lagoon grapes. It is rare. They only produce 4000 bottles a year and the bottles are decorated with just an understated gold leaf hand-battered by a Venetian artisan and baked into the bottle in Murano glass ovens.

It is a curious, thick-skinned golden grape, born in and seemingly tolerant of the salty clay soil and the occasional flood – in the devastatingly high waters of November 2019, I saw photographs of the vineyard and entrance to Venissa submerged under thigh-high seawater, which lasted for several days. It seems to be a really unusual location to make wine, especially in a place that, along with spices and sugar, imported and commercialised wine in the Middle Ages and enjoyed the reputation as the wine capital of the world. Yet, I learned

Above
Harvesting Dorona grapes at Venissa

Right
Venissa

from my visit to Venissa that there are more than 2000 years of wine-making history in Venice – on the islands of Sant'Erasmo, Vignole (aptly named after the word *vigna*, vineyard) and Torcello, for example – and I discovered that vineyards are also found even in the heart of Venice.

San Francesco della Vigna in the Castello district is a Franciscan church named after the vineyard it was built on in 1253. There is still a vineyard there and its wine is being brought back to life thanks to an association called *Laguna nel Bicchiere* ('Lagoon in the glass') that are attempting to recover the lagoon's grapes and make wines from them. They've discovered grapes also from the Camaldolese convent on the island of San Michele, the city's cemetery, where there is Malvasia and Dorona, and from a walled vineyard from the 1500s on the Giudecca from which they produce a natural red wine. They've even made wines from grapes found in the gardens and pergolas of trattorias and *pizzere* in Venice's narrow streets.

While it is expected that monasteries and convents (which often had walled gardens) kept some vineyards, even in private *palazzi*, in Venice, Giampiero Rorato writes of ancient vines scattered throughout the city too in places as central as San Moisè, just steps from Piazza San Marco, as well as San Silvestro, San Benedetto, Sant'Alvisem San Tomà and San Samuele – the last two are right on the Grand Canal.

Smoked tuna, horseradish and artichoke buns

Brioche di tonno affumicato, cren e crema di carciofi

THIS IS A MEMORABLE combination I had while visiting my long-time historian friend Rosa in Venice many years ago. After a foggy, late-morning wander through the maze of laneways from the Zattere to the Rialto market, we had worked up quite an appetite, helped on by the chill in the air. Luckily the Rialto is the place that has had the greatest concentration of *bàcari* and *osterie* since the Renaissance – and where you still find some of Venice's best places for a quick bite to eat.

We had these delicious, pillowy, miniature brioche buns filled with silky slices of smoked tuna, a creamy paste of artichokes and a hint of mustard (this bit of heat is really what makes this) in a little eatery opposite a fish market called Pronto Pesce that now, unfortunately, no longer exists but was surrounded on three sides by fishmongers. You could sit at the big windows and watch the market at its best, fishmongers cleaning squid and oversized seagulls stealing shimmery sardines straight from the counters when the fishmongers turned their backs. Here, they served wonderful seafood *cicchetti* and a restorative, soulful fish broth: no seafood to be seen, but a flavourful, copper-coloured liquid tasting of the sea with tomato and sweet spices.

Makes 2

4–6 artichoke heart quarters preserved in oil
squeeze of lemon juice
1 tablespoon extra-virgin olive oil
2 mini brioche buns
1 teaspoon horseradish cream (or hot English mustard), or to taste
4 slices smoked tuna

Drain the artichokes well and then blend them with the lemon juice and olive oil until you have as smooth or as chunky a paste as you would like. Season with salt to taste.

Slice the buns in half and warm them in a pan, cut side down, until slightly toasted and golden. Spread one side of the bun with ½ teaspoon of the horseradish, followed by a thick layer of artichoke cream, then two slices of smoked tuna and close the panino with the top. Make the second one the same way and serve immediately while the bread is still warm.

VARIATIONS You could use any soft bun for these, or even try them with miniature croissants. If you cannot get smoked tuna, you could use seared fresh tuna, in thin slices, or smoked swordfish or smoked salmon. For a vegetarian version, substitute the tuna with slices of boiled egg, melted Asiago cheese or mozzarella. You really need something that tingles your nose with its heat – hot English mustard or even wasabi would be very good here too.

Roasted capsicum cream and grilled eggplant for little sandwiches

Crema di peperone e melanzane grigliate per francobolli

FOR WHEN A BULGING TRIANGLE of *tramezzino* is just a bit too much, you can find convenient *francobolli*, 'stamps', named for the shape of these small, flat, square-shaped sandwiches. This combination puts together two wonderful preparations that, in themselves, can make other *cicchetti*, paired with halved boiled eggs or freshly cooked prawns (shrimp), on crostini or whatever else you can think of.

This roasted capsicum cream makes approximately 175 g (6 oz/1 cup), which you could also use on baguette or grilled polenta crostini, or as a delicious dip with grissini. The eggplant (aubergine) recipe, too, will make more than you need for the *francobolli*, but this is a preparation that we often have in our fridge, ready to add to a salad, a sandwich or an antipasto platter. It gets better as the days go on, thanks to the marinade.

Makes 4

ROASTED CAPSICUM CREAM
1 red capsicum (bell pepper)
75 g (2¾ oz/⅓ cup) mascarpone, or cream cheese
1 tablespoon olive oil
pinch of dried chilli powder, or to taste
1–2 tablespoons grated parmesan

GRILLED MARINATED EGGPLANT
1 medium eggplant (aubergine)
1 garlic clove, finely chopped
a few parsley sprigs, finely chopped
60 ml (2 fl oz/¼ cup) olive oil

FRANCOBOLLI
2 slices soft sandwich bread, crusts removed
1–1½ tablespoons Roasted capsicum cream (see above)
1 slice Grilled marinated eggplant (see above)

To make the roasted capsicum cream, first roast the entire capsicum, whole, over a fire ideally (you can do this directly on a gas stovetop hob, sitting the pepper right over the flame – a pair of tongs helps – or a barbecue). If you don't have a fire to cook this over, you can also use a dry, very hot pan (cast iron is ideal). You want to blacken it all over and, once it looks completely carbonised (about 20 minutes, or double that if using a pan), place the capsicum in a bowl or container, cover with a lid or tea towel (dish towel) and leave for about 10 minutes to sweat. It should be cool enough to handle by then and you can remove all traces of the burnt skin in a bowl of cool water or under a gentle, steady stream from the tap. Remove the stem, cut open and scoop out the seeds. Then place the capsicum in a food processor and blend with the rest of the ingredients, adding salt to taste. Store in the fridge in an airtight container for up to 4 days.

Slice the eggplant lengthways into 1 cm (½ in) thick slices. Heat a cast-iron (or similar) griddle pan over a medium–high heat and, on a dry pan, cook the slices for about 10 minutes on each side, or until you have nice grill marks and the eggplant slices are juicy and tender. In the meantime, whisk together the garlic, parsley and olive oil with a generous pinch of salt. Pour this over the hot eggplant slices and let them marinate until cool, then, if not using right away, transfer to a container with all the marinade and keep in the fridge for up to 1 week.

To make the francobolli, spread a tablespoon or so of the roasted capsicum cream thickly onto a slice of bread, add a slice of the grilled eggplant and top with a slice of bread. Cut into four small squares for four cicchetti. These are lovely just as is, or you can also toast them until the bread is golden brown on both sides – an electric sandwich press is ideal, otherwise use a dry frying pan and keep a firm weight on the sandwich (press down with a spatula, for example, or find a slightly-too-small lid and place that on top).

VARIATIONS You can use zucchini (courgette) instead of eggplant. If you like, you can add a splash of red-wine vinegar to the eggplant marinade, or some fresh herbs such as basil or mint.

Tramezzini di gamberetti e rucola

VENETIAN TRAMEZZINI ARE A SIGHT to behold. Quite different from the classic Turin-style *tramezzini*, which were invented in 1926 and look more like English tea sandwiches, the lagoon version is a carefully made work of art where the bulging domed filling is held in with tightly sealed edges of the softest, crustless sandwich bread.

Supposedly coined by the poet and politician Gabriele D'Annunzio, the word *tramezzino* comes from *intramezzo*, meaning in between – in fact, a *tramezzino* in Venice, which is usually sold as a triangle, not as a full sandwich, is the perfect bite for in between meals, or as part of an aperitivo in the evening with a glass of wine. It even makes a delicious breakfast in lieu of the sweet offerings at pastry shops.

For those passionate about *tramezzini*, you should make a note to visit these rather nondescript, humble, very simple cafes that specialise in sandwiches, in particular the classic Venetian-style *tramezzini* bursting with more fillings than you could imagine: Bar ai Nomboli (San Polo), Bar Rialto da Lollo (San Polo), Bar alla Toletta (Dorsoduro) and Bar Tiziano near the Rialto. I also love the elegant display of *tramezzini* at the historic pastry shop Rosa Salva in Campo Santi Giovanni e Paolo (San Marco), where I'm always tempted by their daily offerings, maybe the one with giardiniera pickles, anchovies and hard-boiled egg, or the creamy chicken salad on brown bread.

Some favourite fillings you might find here and elsewhere as you wander the streets of Venice include crab meat with rocket (arugula), pumpkin and porchetta, smoked beef, asparagus and gorgonzola, prawn (shrimp) and artichokes, mortadella and provolone cheese, *baccalà mantecato* and radicchio, salmon and egg, tuna with tomato and capers, prosciutto and whole boiled eggs or mushrooms, even very traditional fillings, such as radicchio and *sfilacci di cavallo* (horse meat; Bar alla Toletta does this). The key in all of these fillings is abundant mayonnaise to hold everything together.

NOTE In Italy you can easily find the perfect, very soft *tramezzino* bread at supermarkets – it comes in packs, sliced lengthways, so as long as a loaf of bread, no more than 1 cm (½ in) thick and already crustless. Softness is key in getting the dome shape and well-sealed edges without the bread cracking. If you don't have this ideal bread, use any soft sandwich bread (white or wholemeal), but there are a couple of tricks you can keep up your sleeve to ensure a good shape. One, before you begin, sprinkle the bread with a tiny amount of water to dampen slightly (if you have a handy plain water spray bottle this works well) and then use a rolling pin to lightly roll the bread out a little and make it a bit thinner, a bit more pliable. If not serving the *tramezzini* right away, keep them in an airtight container so the bread does not dry out, or covered with a slightly damp tea towel (dish towel) and store in the fridge.

*Makes 2 sandwiches that could serve 4
as antipasto or as cicchetti*

1 tablespoon extra-virgin olive oil
150 g (5½ oz) fresh school prawns
    (shrimp), shelled
1 small garlic clove, finely chopped
3 tablespoons mayonnaise
4 slices soft sandwich bread, crusts
    removed; see Note
handful of rocket (arugula), shredded

Heat the olive oil in a small saucepan over a medium heat. Add the prawns and garlic and toss so that the prawns cook on all sides. These small Venetian prawns take about 1 minute to turn completely opaque and curled. Set aside in a small bowl to cool. Strain them if necessary, then add 1½–2 tablespoons of the mayonnaise, or just enough so that they are well coated, then season with some pepper.

Place the bread on a work surface and spread all the slices right to the edges with the rest of the mayonnaise. Spoon half of the prawn mixture onto one slice, concentrating it in the middle of the slice and leaving a border of 1 cm (½ in) all around. Do the same on a second slice. On top of the prawns, place half of the shredded rocket in another layer, then repeat on the second slice. Top the rocket with a slice of bread, mayonnaise side down, and when you do this, cup your hand over the filling, while pushing down on the edges. Your aim is to 'seal' the tramezzino on all edges with the mayonnaise while at the same time having a bulging, filled centre. Keeping this shape, cut the tramezzino into two triangles. Repeat with the other tramezzino.

VARIATIONS This classic combination is made with tiny school prawns (shrimp), which can be found already shelled. You could substitute them with regular prawns, but they will need an extra minute of cooking.

A canal in Cannaregio

Tramezzini di asparagi e uova

Tramezzini di asparagi e uova

IF YOU ASK ME, boiled eggs are the perfect filling for a *tramezzino* (pictured on page 97); you only need to accompany them with a seasonal vegetable, or perhaps your favourite *salumi* or preserved fish, and you have the ideal sandwich. Asparagus and eggs are a wonderful combination, if anything because they are traditionally abundant at the exact same time – spring – so it's natural to pair them together.

Makes 2 sandwiches that could serve 4 as antipasto or cicchetti

handful of thin asparagus
2 hard-boiled eggs (see page 77)
2 tablespoons mayonnaise
4 slices soft sandwich bread, crusts
    removed (see Note on page 94)

VARIATION If using thick asparagus, you should slice them in half lengthways before proceeding. If asparagus is not in season, you could consider using another fresh seasonal vegetable – try thinly sliced radicchio, sliced tomatoes, grilled slices of eggplant (aubergine) or zucchini (courgette). Otherwise, marinated artichoke hearts are great here too.

Break off and discard the woody ends then cook the asparagus in boiling water with a good pinch of salt for 3 minutes, or until they are bright green and tender (thicker asparagus, even halved, may need a further 2–3 minutes). Set aside to cool then cut them a little shorter than the length of the bread slices.

In a small bowl, mash the peeled, boiled eggs with a good pinch of salt and 2 teaspoons of the mayonnaise, saving the rest for the bread.

Place the bread on a work surface and spread all the slices right to the edges with a teaspoon of mayonnaise each. Place a layer of asparagus onto a slice of bread, leaving a 1 cm (½ in) border all around. Add 2 tablespoons or so of the egg in the centre on top of the asparagus layer. Cover with a slice of bread, mayonnaise side down, and when you do this, cup your hand over the filling while pushing down on the edges. Your aim is to 'seal' the tramezzino on all edges with the mayonnaise while at the same time having a bulging, filled centre. Keeping this shape, cut the tramezzino into two triangles. Repeat with the other tramezzino, then serve immediately.

Crostini with radicchio and walnut cream

Crostini con crema di radicchio e noci

THIS DELICIOUS CREAM, much like the Roasted capsicum cream (page 92), could be used for many different *cicchetti* preparations, for *tramezzini* or even as a dip with crunchy vegetables. It's also delicious stirred through a pasta or risotto. The lemon juice here helps enhance and preserve that intense colour that makes radicchio the most beautiful vegetable that exists, so don't leave it out. If you don't have mascarpone, try using thick natural yoghurt (like Greek yoghurt) or cream cheese, but also stracchino, a creamy, very fresh cheese, or robiola, from the same cheese family, are wonderful, slightly tangy, creamy options here. Another cheese you may want to try if you like its strong flavour is gorgonzola. With the slightly bitter radicchio, it's a match made in heaven. You can use pine nuts instead of the walnuts.

Makes enough for about 12–15 crostini

1 small round head of radicchio di
    Chioggia (otherwise use half)
1 garlic clove, peeled but left whole
2 tablespoons olive oil
juice of ½ lemon
2 tablespoons walnuts, chopped, plus
    more for garnish
60 g (2 oz/4 tablespoons) mascarpone
crostini, to serve

Peel off any rough outer leaves of the radicchio and discard (these tend to be bitter). Chop off the stem and wash the leaves then roughly chop them – no need to dry them. Place the garlic clove in a wide frying pan with the olive oil and heat gently, allowing the oil to infuse with the garlic. Don't let it brown too much; a few minutes of gentle sizzling should do it. Remove the garlic clove then add the radicchio, along with the lemon juice and a good pinch of salt. Toss together over a medium heat until the radicchio begins to wilt, about 3–5 minutes. Remove from the heat and let it cool, then blend in a food processor until smooth. If you like a very smooth cream, add the walnuts to this too, but if you prefer a bit of texture, leave them out until the very end and simply stir through. Add the mascarpone and taste for seasoning (you may like an extra squeeze of lemon or some freshly ground pepper), giving it one final blend to combine well.

Spread over bread or crostini of your choice (toasted or untoasted baguette slices, or on grilled polenta), and if you like, top with some chopped walnuts. Store leftovers in an airtight container for up to 3 days in the fridge.

Radicchio, the flower of winter

FORCED RADICCHIO IS A BEAUTIFUL, extremely versatile salad vegetable, a star of the favourite produce of the Veneto, along with asparagus. 'It looks like a fleshy purple flower, as fresh as if it had been specially created to bring spring to the dinner table in winter', wrote Ada Boni in her *Italian Regional Cooking* cookbook.

There are many different varieties of radicchio, usually named after their city of origin, and they each have different qualities, which are appreciated for different uses in the kitchen, although what they tend to have in common are juicy, bitter leaves and pretty colours.

The most well known are radicchio di Chioggia, a round, ruby red salad head, slightly less bitter than its relatives, from the eponymous town south of Venice, and radicchio di Treviso, an elongated variety from just north of Venice, which actually comes in two forms and is protected by IGP (Indication of Geographic Protection) status. In its *precoce*, or early-harvest form, in autumn, it has an elongated shape, but when you find it in its highly prized *tardivo*, or late-harvest form, its leaves have transformed with the most impossible, almost tentacle-like curls of crunchy, bright, white-veined ruby leaves.

To earn their IGP status, both *precoce* and *tardivo* must be grown only in a select number of municipalities in the provinces of Treviso, Padova or Venice. *Tardivo* is considered the king of the radicchio family. It doesn't just grow like this but takes weeks of manual work. The seeds are planted in fields in the height of summer, then once the first frosts of autumn come along (there should be two frosts for IGP standards), the leaves are 'burned' and growth is stopped. This is usually in late November and is where the transformation begins – the radicchio is taken, roots and all, and transferred to large pools of running water at a constant temperature in complete darkness for 10–25 days. The water revives the plant and it begins to grow again. Without sunlight and without photosynthesis turning the leaves green, the characteristic brilliant red and white leaves grow. The plant is then trimmed and cleaned manually (a process called *toelettatura*), removing about 70 per cent of the dead and wilted outer leaves and trimming the root to retain just the heart of the plant. It is then thoroughly washed and packed, ready for the market. It's in season in the coldest months of winter, until the end of February.

Meanwhile the regular Treviso *precoce*, which is a little sweeter than the later-harvest versions, is a wonderful variety to cook with (I love it grilled or *in saor*, see page 61), and is harvested from September. Its characteristic elongated form is created in the fields, with an elastic band wrapped around the tops of each broad salad head like '*soldatini*', 'soldiers', which keeps the hearts of the salad blanketed in darkness for 15–20 days so that, like the *tardivo*, the lack of photosynthesis keeps the new leaves from turning green. When they are harvested, they are cleaned in the field of their outer green leaves to reveal their red hearts.

Then there are the rose-like speckled pink and creamy hued tender leaves of radicchio variegato Castelfranco, which is almost too pretty to eat and my favourite salad.

I love radicchio deliciously dressed in something sweet–acidic to balance its slight bitterness. This is one very rare occasion where I like balsamic vinegar in salad, particularly a sweeter, aged one. It's also very nice with a hit of something mustardy (like the dressing of the *Insalata di Gallina Padovana*, page 158) or with something strong and salty (perfect with prosciutto, anchovies or herring; try the *Insalata di aringa grigliata*, page 156). And it goes marvellously well with cheese – gorgonzola ticks the salty/strong/spicy boxes all at once.

Crostini with mackerel, olives and pine nuts

Crostini con sgombro, olive e pinoli

I HAVE HAD SOMETHING like this in a humble *bàcaro* and wine shop called Cantina Aziende Agricole while on my way to meet friends on the busy *fondamenta* just over the bridge. It's a good stop with simple *cicchetti* but plenty of choice, especially fried things. The original is with tuna, but I think that tinned mackerel, which is so flavourful and undervalued, makes a very delicious *cicchetto* (and is equally good as a *tramezzino* filling) livened up with olives and pine nuts. It's important here to have very delicious olives; I would go with black marinated olives such as kalamata, or taggiasca olives (these are very small, so use double the amount). If they've already been pitted, then half the work is done here; otherwise, use the flat side of a large kitchen knife to squash the olives and then you can pull the pits out easily.

VARIATIONS Try this with tuna, or another favourite tinned fish, with walnuts instead of the pine nuts (or leave them out), and with any olives that you prefer. The classic chopped garlic and a few sprigs of finely chopped parsley would be a good addition too.

Makes 6 cicchetti

90 g (3 oz) tinned mackerel, drained
1 tablespoon pine nuts, finely chopped
6 large, good-quality marinated olives, pitted and finely chopped
1–2 tablespoons mayonnaise, or to taste
1 tablespoon olive oil, or as needed
a few parsley leaves, finely chopped
6 thick baguette slices, or other crusty bread
pickled baby onions or capers in brine, for garnish

Combine the mackerel, pine nuts and olives in a bowl, breaking the mackerel up with a fork. Add the mayonnaise and enough olive oil (try a tablespoon at first) to mash the mixture into a rough paste. If you prefer this smooth like a cream, you can do it in a food processor instead. Taste for seasoning and add pepper if you like but you won't need salt; I find mackerel is usually flavourful enough. Mix through the parsley and spread onto toasted or untoasted baguette slices. Garnish with a baby onion (my preference) or a caper on top.

Cured sea bass with cumin

Branzino marinato al cumino

SERVED ON WARM CROSTINI with butter, this fragrant cured sea bass seems to melt in your mouth and is an absolute treat for the senses. This brilliant dish is inspired by a recipe in the Slow Food–produced cookbook, *Ricette di Osterie del Veneto*, from Ristorante Al Vecchio Marina on the Lido of Jesolo, a 15-km (9-mile) long beach north-east of Venice. I found it so intriguing because of the use of a spice like cumin, which is rare in Italian cuisine, but it is so perfectly suited to this dish, and also for the choice to cure a fish such as sea bass, which in Venice is prized for its delicate flesh and is traditionally roasted or boiled for very special occasions, such as Christmas Eve. The original recipe has fresh lemon balm (*melissa*) leaves decorating it too, but I prefer the spices; a pinch of cumin and some pink peppercorn is lovely. You need to begin this recipe at least 2 days before you want to serve it (5 days, according to the original recipe, but I cannot wait that long).

Makes 20 cicchetti

1 × 1 kg (2 lb 3 oz) whole sea bass, or
  2 sea bass fillets, scaled but skin on,
  about 800 g (1 lb 12 oz)
120 g (4½ oz) coarse salt
120 g (4½ oz) raw sugar
juice of 1 lemon
1 teaspoon honey
1 teaspoon cumin seeds, crushed, plus a
  pinch for garnish
2–3 tablespoons extra-virgin olive oil
20 baguette slices
1 garlic clove
butter, softened

To fillet the whole fish, first make a diagonal slice that almost cuts the head off and follows the opening of the gills. From here you will cut the first fillet by locating the backbone and, using the spine as a guide, cut all the way along the length of the fish to the tail and pull out the first fillet. Now flip the fish over and repeat. You should be left with a head and bones and tail all attached. This makes the most wonderful stock for a fish soup or a fish risotto, so set it aside for boiling with a carrot, onion and celery, then strain – this freezes well. Otherwise, ask your fishmonger to fillet it for you (and if you would like to keep the rest for stock, do tell them that you want to keep it for that purpose).

Gently run the fillets under cold water then pat them dry. Combine the salt and sugar and sprinkle about half of this mixture in a glass or ceramic dish, place the fillets on top, skin side up, then cover completely with the rest of the sugar and salt mixture. Place in the fridge to cure for 24 hours.

The next day, remove the fish from the curing mixture, gently rinse and pat dry. Place in a new, clean glass or ceramic dish. Combine the lemon juice with the honey and cumin and pour this over the fish and leave to marinate for another 24 hours.

Remove the fish from the marinade and pat dry gently. Slice the fish on a slight diagonal; you want to do this as thinly as possible and then discard the skin. Dress the cured fish with a generous drizzle of very good olive oil and some crushed pink or black pepper, and another pinch of cumin. Cover and leave to rest until ready for serving. (It can be kept like this for at least 3 days in the fridge).

When ready to serve, toast the baguette rounds and rub each once with a fresh garlic clove before buttering them, all while the bread is still warm. Place a slice of cured sea bass on top and serve immediately.

Tuna tartare

Tartare di tonno

IT'S ONLY NATURAL that in a city where seafood is such an important part of the cuisine that a rather international but very popular preparation like tuna tartare has become a common sight in Venetian *bàcari*. In the Dorsoduro quarter of Venice, Cantina del Vino già Schiavi (also known as Cantinone or al Bottegon) serves a particularly loved *cicchetto* of tuna tartare with bitter cocoa. Cantinone is one of the best examples of a classic *bàcaro* serving a dizzying array of *cicchetti* on generously thick slices of baguette made by Alessandra De Respini, as she has for decades.

This is a more classic combination of flavours inspired by what you might find on a traditional beef tartare, but it works so well with tuna – the anchovies provide a great boost of flavour and I think they are a must, but if any anchovy-haters decide to leave them out, just make sure to adjust the seasoning appropriately. I am personally very fond of the lemon zest and capers in this.

Makes 8 cicchetti

200 g (7 oz) sashimi-grade raw tuna
2 anchovies preserved in oil, finely chopped
2 teaspoons capers, rinsed, finely chopped, plus extra for garnish
zest and juice of 1 lemon
1 tablespoon extra-virgin olive oil
8 toasted baguette slices

With a very sharp knife, chop the tuna into small dice, about 5 mm (¼ in) wide and set aside in a bowl. In a separate small bowl, combine the anchovies, capers, lemon zest and half of the juice to start with, and the olive oil. Season to taste with salt and freshly ground black pepper then mix this dressing through the tuna. Taste and adjust for seasoning – you may like a little more lemon juice or another pinch of salt. Spoon onto toasted baguette slices and add a caper on top as a garnish.

NOTE Serve immediately – or quite soon after making this. If you leave the lemon juice dressing on too long, the raw fish will begin to cure, which changes the texture, so if you want to prepare this ahead of time, I would recommend keeping the seasoning separate from the prepared tartare and mixing them just before serving.

VARIATION You could use sashimi-grade salmon instead of the tuna.

Carrot mostarda with mustard and roast ham

Mostarda di carote con senape e prosciutto arrosto

THIS CURIOUS CARROT MOSTARDA was one of the first recipes from Mariù Salvatori de Zuliani's cookbook that I wanted to cook. She describes this as an old recipe to make in the month of September, using many lemons and much, much more sugar and a low, slow, 4-hour cooking time. She pairs this with boiled meat, as mostarda often is. I think it is lovely with prosciutto arrosto or prosciutto cotto, which is cooked ham as opposed to cured as prosciutto crudo is. Use a top-quality, freshly sliced, off-the-bone ham.

You could also see this as a sort of *in saor* recipe (see *Radicchio in saor*, page 61) if you perhaps leave out the sugar, but add raisins and pine nuts to it for sweetness – in fact, this is another Venetian Jewish recipe recounted in the Slow Food *Ricette di Osteria del Veneto*, a dish for celebrating the New Year for the symbolic happy golden colour and shape of the carrot slices.

This will make enough mostarda for twelve *cicchetti*. But if you have any leftovers, try it out next to a roast or on sandwiches – also see Variations, below, for more ideas.

VARIATIONS You could substitute the roast ham with roast beef or, for a vegetarian version, try the carrot mostarda with gorgonzola or another strong blue cheese (skipping the mustard and mascarpone). I had something similar at the popular *bàcaro* Vino Vero – a warm crostino topped with mostarda and a slice of gooey washed-rind cheese.

Makes 290 g (10 oz/1 cup), or a small jar of mostarda

CARROT MOSTARDA
400 g (14 oz) carrots, peeled and thinly sliced
zest and juice of 2 lemons
2 tablespoons red-wine vinegar
100 g (3½ oz) sugar

TO ASSEMBLE EACH CICCHETTO
1 thick slice fresh or toasted baguette, for crostini
¼ teaspoon hot English mustard, or to taste
2 tablespoons mascarpone, or cream cheese
1 tablespoon Carrot mostarda (see above)
1 thin slice roast ham

Combine the carrots, lemon zest and juice and vinegar in a small saucepan with 500 ml (17 fl oz/2 cups) water and bring to the boil. Add the sugar and, once it has dissolved, turn the heat to a low simmer, cover, and let cook slowly for 1–1½ hours. The carrots should be soft and the liquid should be reduced and syrupy. Once made, the mostarda keeps well, like home-made jam, in an airtight jar in the fridge.

To assemble the cicchetti, on each slice of bread spread the mustard, followed by the mascarpone, then the carrot mostarda and top with a slice of roast ham.

Prawns wrapped in lardo

Gamberi e lardo

THIS IS DELICIOUSLY SALTY, thanks to the lardo, so it begs for a nice drink to go along with it, and it's so incredibly simple that you can make this almost as quickly as it will be devoured. Use very large, very fresh, very beautiful prawns (shrimp) for this. If you cannot find lardo – which is spiced and fragrant and should be shaved paper thin like prosciutto – you can, as a second choice, use prosciutto or pancetta instead, but it should be paper thin so as not to overwhelm the sweet, fleshy prawns.

Makes 6 cicchetti

6 king prawns (shrimp)
6 basil leaves
6 slices lardo

Peel the body of the prawns – for aesthetics, I like to leave the head and tail, or, at the very least, just the tail which is a useful tool for picking up with fingers. If you prefer, you can remove both. Devein the prawns, if necessary, with a sharp knife along the ridge of the body and pull out the vein. Wrap a basil leaf around the body, then a thin strip of lardo. Continue with the rest.

Heat a heavy-bottomed frying pan such as a cast-iron or non-stick pan (something you would cook a steak in, for example) over a high heat then cook the prawns, turning once, until they turn opaque and bright orange and you see the lardo turn transparent and the green of the basil shine through. It should only take 1½ minutes total. No need for salt or oil here; the lardo is flavourful and fatty enough. Serve immediately.

Above
Giant prawns for *Gamberi e lardo*
(page 111)

Left
The Ponte del Megio, which leads to
Calle del Spezier, named for the spice
trader that was once here

Fritti
Fritti
Fritti

Fritti
Fried cicchetti

Calamari fritti
Fried calamari

Fiori di zucca ripieni di baccalà mantecato
Fried zucchini flowers stuffed with whipped cod

Mozzarella in carrozza alla veneziana
Venetian-style fried mozzarella sandwiches

Tondini di formaggio
Fried cheese rounds

Polpette di carne
Fried meatballs

Polpette di baccalà
Cod fritters

Baccalà fritto
Battered fried salt cod

Schie fritte
Fried Venetian prawns

Zucchine impanate
Crumbed zucchini

The art of frying

Fried foods have long made up a favourite part of any round of *cicchetti* in Venice – especially just-fried, on-the-spot kind of treats that are worth waiting and lining up for (see the *Polpette di carne*, page 130). Sandro Brandolisio describes the *Fritureta* or *fritturina* of mixed fried fish (see *Calamari fritti*, page 122) in his book about *cicchetti* during the 1950s and 60s as the classic street food that you could find in Venice at many *bàcari*. Fried on the spot and sold piping hot and wrapped in paper, perhaps with a piece of fried polenta tucked in there too, you would walk and eat and chat until you finished and immediately headed for the closest *bàcaro* for a glass of wine or two to wash it all down.

But there is one fried treat that is particularly loved and symbolic of Venice's cuisine – *fritole*, or sweet fritters (see page 202). For centuries, these fried treats were the number-one street food, sold by peddlers who roamed Venice on foot, setting up their pots of oil and cooking on street corners to passers-by. These *fritoleri*, as the fritter-makers were known, had formed a guild, *l'arte dei fritoleri*, in Venice as early as 1609. According to Elio Zorzi in his book *Osterie Veneziane*, there were seventy members at this time, each with a particular district of Venice assigned to them by the guild. It was a trade reserved exclusively for Venetians, and one that was passed on only to heirs.

The Venetian printmaker Gaetano Zompini is best remembered for his collection of sixty etchings from 1746–1754, *Le Arti che Vanno per Via*, depicting *fritoleri* along with other common peddlers, artisans and merchants who could be found selling their goods on foot (or by gondola) around Venice, from the egg seller and the glassmaker (who will even take broken glass), to the fresh ricotta vendor and the clam seller (already purged and ready to cook). Each worker is depicted with one or two other characters in classically Venetian settings: under porticoes, beside bridges, with the typical *calli*, or narrow streets, and bell towers etched into the backgrounds like theatre backdrops, and the etchings are accompanied by short poems in Venetian dialect written by Zompini's friend, the priest Questini. They are a charming, extraordinary account of everyday life in eighteenth-century Venice.

Some of the merchants are quite specific – the ink and rat poison seller, for example, the one selling foraged herbs, or beef blood sausage, the one who goes door to door with vinegar or arrives by gondola with wood. One of my favourites depicts *fritole* – fritters – being fried by a seated woman concentrating on a huge pan over an open fire. At her feet is a wooden barrel filled with batter. A noblewoman waiting for her order of fritters, which are being strung on a skewer by a young boy, fans the billowing smoke away from her face, while her companion leans towards her, pointing his finger out of the scene, as if to say, 'We'll take them to go!'

How to deep-fry

Many people shy away from deep-frying at home, but it is simple and doesn't have to be messy. We do it very often at home and, over the years, I've come to adapt a system that I find works really well for my family. Unless I am making a huge batch of something (rare), I usually fry in my smallest frying pan. The reason for this is simply because using a smaller pan means I can use less oil. Because fried foods are so quick to cook, I can fry in batches and serve the entire plate and everything is still hot – and, in the case of particularly hungry people, they eat as I fry!

Frying at the right temperature is really important; it will ensure you have a deliciously crisp outer crust while not being greasy. I used to carefully measure my oil with a candy thermometer to make sure I had the right temperature (about 160°C/320°F for something that takes a bit longer to cook through, such as dough, like in the *fritole*, or a thicker fish like the *baccalà fritto*, to between 170–180°C/340–350°F for things that are much quicker to cook, such as calamari or zucchini/courgette flowers – but not any hotter than that). If the oil begins smoking you have definitely exceeded the limit and you should really avoid it getting to this point; it is unsafe for your kitchen but also the oil begins to degrade at this temperature and it will affect the flavour of your food.

But I have learned over the years to recognise visual cues to know when the oil is ready. It will start to look like it is shimmering and snaking through the pan. But my favourite trick is to dip the end of a wooden spoon or my chopstick (I fry with a pair of extra-long Japanese chopsticks; they are the best for delicately plucking things out of oil, but you can also use a slotted spoon or tongs, if you are careful that the metal ends don't dig into the delicate crust of batter, or a spider, which is like a steel net on the end of a long handle) and on contact the wood will immediately be surrounded by tiny, very energetic bubbles.

My preferred vegetable oil to use for frying is organic sunflower oil. Seed oils such as sunflower oil have a very high smoke point and are neutral in flavour. But you can use any vegetable oil, even olive oil if it is all that you have (light or refined olive oil has a high smoke point more or less equal to seed oil – however, if it's the kind of good, unrefined extra-virgin olive oil that is thick and deep green and you'd only dare eat it raw, drizzled on your very best bread, I wouldn't recommend it for frying simply because it would be a shame, but also because extra-virgin olive oil has a very low smoke point so you need to be careful with your temperature).

Some people filter used frying oil and reuse it for further frying, but I personally do not reuse vegetable oil after it has cooled and I would not recommend it. The quality of the oil will degrade, and will become potentially carcinogenic if it has not been carefully temperature controlled or has gone over its smoke point. The smoke point of any oil will lower after it has cooled and so you will also need to be more careful the next time you use it, making it less reliable to fry with – not to mention it will also become rancid pretty quickly. So, I avoid reusing it for cooking with, though I always make sure to dispose of used frying oil correctly and take it to my local recycling centre (see page 121 for how to do this).

A few extra tips

Have everything ready before you start; frying is quick! A wire cooling rack lined with absorbent kitchen paper is an ideal surface for putting your just-fried food on to drain of any excess oil. If you don't have a cooling rack, try a wooden chopping board; it absorbs any excess moisture better than a plate, a plastic board or stone surface. Remember to change the kitchen paper when it gets too oily.

Fry a few pieces at a time to avoid overcrowding the pan, which would lower the oil's temperature and lead to a soggy, greasy crust – a good rule of thumb is to fill the pan halfway (or two-thirds, if you must, but no more).

If the oil is not quite as deep as you thought, or you're at the end of the batch and it is running low, you can always top it up – just remember to wait for the oil to return to the right temperature before frying.

If salting, salt the food as soon as you take it out of the pan and place it on the paper. If you salt when it's had a chance to cool a bit, it will simply fall off. The same goes for sugar, in the case of the *fritole* – don't wait, roll them in the sugar as soon as you can so that it attaches nicely.

If you want to fry multiple types of food while you have the oil hot and ready, you can absolutely fry different things in the same pan but do them one at a time and in a particular order. If frying something with a delicate flavour (or sweet, such as the *fritole*), I would begin with those first – and fry the fish, for example, last. I would also give priority to battered foods, while doing the crumbed foods at the end to avoid having burnt crumbs stuck to the batter. In between each dish (indeed, even between each batch), make sure to scoop out any debris with a slotted spoon or a spider.

A note on disposing of frying oil

In many regions in Italy where deep-frying is popular, councils have special bins for disposing of used vegetable oil safely, where it has the chance to be filtered and recycled into other products. Look into your own council's regulations for how to dump or recycle frying oil responsibly. Do not pour used oil, even in small amounts, down your drain; it can cause serious plumbing issues and contribute to water pollution. Instead, let it cool then pour it into a sealable container such as a plastic bottle or glass jar and keep it, topping it up every time you fry, until it is full, then you can take it to your council disposal easily. If you don't have a large amount of oil or don't fry often, there are two other options. You can wipe it out with kitchen paper and compost or dispose of it normally and, if you have compost, you can also compost frying oil. Just be sure it is not a large amount and to mix it in thoroughly; adding too much at once can slow down the composting process.

Fried calamari

Calamari fritti

THIS MIGHT JUST BE the ultimate warm-weather *cicchetto*. Just-fried, too hot to touch, you can often find fried calamari at a *bàcaro* strung on a skewer together, or sold in yellow paper cones, and it needs nothing more than a glass of cold, bubbly Prosecco next to it. You can also find this as *fritto misto*, mixed fried seafood, which might include pieces of fish or whole tiny fish known as *latterini* or *atherine*, and crunchy whole prawns (shrimp), to be eaten head and all. But we are particularly fond of calamari; it is my daughters' favourite. The trick to this very simple dish is to have very fresh, small calamari and to fry in small batches – not crowding the pan keeps the oil hot, which means a crunchy coating.

Serves 4 as cicchetti

350 g (12½ oz) calamari (about 2 small calamari)
60 g (2 oz/4 tablespoons) plain (all-purpose) flour
vegetable oil, for frying

Rinse the calamari and make sure they are cleaned. If the fishmonger did not do it for you, you can clean them by pulling off the head; use just the tentacles and cut off the part with the eyes. Pull out the beak, which you will find in the middle of the tentacles. Reach into the body and carefully pull out the glassy, plastic-like quill inside and any guts or ink sac. Pull off the wings and, as you do that, you should be able to now easily pull off all the skin, which is like a very thin membrane. Rinse well, so you have just an empty white tube and the tentacles.

Cut the calamari into 1.5–2 cm (½–¾ in) rings. You can leave the tentacles as they are or cut in half lengthways. Coat them completely in the flour (sometimes it helps to coat them first entirely in half of the flour, then follow with the rest of the flour and toss again).

Place enough vegetable oil in a small, deep-frying pan or saucepan so that it is at least 3 cm (1¼ in) deep and bring to a medium heat (about 170°C/340°F if you have a candy thermometer). When it is hot enough, the surface of the oil should look as if it is shimmering. The bottom of a wooden spoon inserted in the oil should immediately be surrounded by energetic, tiny bubbles. Drop several pieces of calamari into the hot oil (but not too many at once; you want the pan to be no more than half full) and turn halfway through if needed, until the flour coating is a light golden colour and crisp-looking, about 1 minute total. Drain on kitchen paper and immediately sprinkle with salt. Continue with the rest of the calamari and serve while hot.

Fried zucchini flowers stuffed with whipped cod

Fiori di zucca ripieni di baccalà mantecato

THIS IS AN ABSOLUTELY DELICIOUS dish that is really just another way to eat fried cod (and happens to be handy if you have any leftover *Baccalà mantecato*, page 46). You could easily double or triple this recipe, but if there are only two or three of you, this will be enough; they are deceptively filling! These flowers are particularly good when eaten while piping hot, so I suggest frying them while your guests are eagerly waiting to eat them.

Makes 6 cicchetti

50 g (1¾ oz/⅓ cup) plain (all-purpose) flour
6 zucchini (courgette) flowers (about 60 g/2 oz)
180 g (6½ oz/6 tablespoons) Baccalà mantecato (page 46)
vegetable oil, for frying

Make the batter by whisking the flour with 125 ml (4 fl oz/½ cup) chilled water to a smooth, runny batter. Place in the fridge and let the batter chill completely. Meanwhile, prepare the zucchini flowers by gently opening the petals and removing the stamen or stigma inside the flower by pulling or cutting it off. Set aside.

Measure out 1 tablespoon of baccalà mantecato for each flower, shaping them into thick logs with your hands (or make quenelles using two spoons) and placing them inside the flowers, folding the petals back over the baccalà to enclose it. When all the flowers have been filled and you're ready to fry, pour the vegetable oil into a deep-frying pan or a small saucepan – ideally the oil should be deep enough so that when you put the flowers in they will be fully submerged, about 7.5 cm (3 in).

Heat over a medium heat to 160°C (320°F). If you don't have a candy thermometer, there are some cues to look for: the oil should begin to shimmer and the bottom of a wooden spoon inserted in the oil should immediately be surrounded by energetic, tiny bubbles. One at a time, dip the flowers into the chilled batter, ensuring a good, thick coating particularly around the opening (I like to twist the petals together slightly at the opening to help close them), and then place carefully in the hot oil. Continue with the zucchini flowers until you can comfortably fit them into the pan without overcrowding (you may need to do this in two batches if your pan is small) and fry for about 2½–3 minutes, or until the batter is crisp and pale golden.

Remove and drain on kitchen paper, then sprinkle with salt while piping hot. Continue frying, if you have done batches, and serve while hot.

VARIATIONS For a vegetarian version, substitute the *baccalà* with mozzarella or ricotta seasoned with lemon zest, salt and some parmesan. Or simply fry the zucchini (courgette) flowers just as they are dipped in batter (and this would be vegan). I often do this if I have a mountain of flowers and I've run out of *baccalà*.

Fritti

Mozzarella in carrozza alla veneziana

THESE DEEP-FRIED SANDWICHES may have been invented in Naples in the nineteenth century, but dipping bread in a mixture of egg and milk and frying it is an old tradition in many places, and this is a fried *cicchetto* that Venetians have made entirely their own. The classic Neapolitan one is made with stale bread, and the mozzarella sandwiches are dipped first in flour, then in plain beaten egg and, finally, in breadcrumbs. But Edda Servi Machlin, who was born in the heart of the Jewish quarter of the Tuscan town of Pitigliano, has a recipe in *The Classic Cuisine of the Italian Jews* (1981) where she mixes egg, milk and flour into a batter and submerges the sandwiches into this before deep-frying. This is similar to the way you'll find them also in Venice, such as at the Rosticceria Gilson near the Rialto bridge, where they are made in enormous quantities, and also in the historic *bàcaro* Cantina Do Spade – it is at the latter where they explain the other important difference in the Venetian-style sandwich: they use the softest sandwich bread, like what you would make *tramezzini* (see pages 94 and 98) with – and they are served in two ways: with anchovies or with prosciutto cotto, ham.

Makes 6 cicchetti

1–2 balls fresh mozzarella, approximately 150 g (5½ oz)
1 egg, separated
80 ml (2½ fl oz/⅓ cup) well-chilled full-cream (whole) milk
75 g (2¾ oz/½ cup) plain (all-purpose) flour
6 anchovies preserved in oil, drained, or ham
6 slices sandwich bread, crusts removed and cut into 2 rectangles
vegetable oil, for frying

NOTE I don't tend to add salt to these because the anchovy or ham adds enough, but if you decide not to use either for a vegetarian version they will be a little more delicate so you may like a little sprinkle of salt. I prefer salting them when they are just fried.

Slice the mozzarella balls into 1 cm (½ in) thick discs, then drain them in one layer over a sieve lined with some absorbent kitchen paper while you prepare the batter.

In a small bowl, whip the egg white with a whisk until it is foamy. In another bowl, whisk together the yolk and the milk and then add the flour, until you have a smooth batter. Add the egg whites gently and keep it chilled while you make the sandwiches.

Place a slice of mozzarella and an anchovy between two rectangles of bread and continue with the other slices so that you have six rectangular sandwiches.

Heat the oil in a frying pan, about 2–3 cm (¾–1¼ in) deep, over a medium heat until it reaches 170°C (340°F) (see page 118 for visual cues if you don't have a candy thermometer). One at a time, submerge the bread into the chilled batter to cover all over, lightly squish the edges together

as you do so, and then gently place in the oil with the help of a slotted spoon. Fry for about 90 seconds, turning once so it is evenly golden brown all over. Place on absorbent kitchen paper to drain and salt them immediately. You could fry two at a time. Continue with the rest of the sandwiches.

They're delicious freshly fried when still hot and the cheese has melted, but honestly, these are so good I would (and do) eat them cold too. These also do very well made several hours ahead of time and simply reheated in the oven, coming out as if they had just been freshly fried. Let them cool completely before putting in an airtight container and keeping in the fridge until you need them. Then place them on a lined baking tray in the oven at 180°C (350°F) and heat until they are piping hot.

Fried cheese rounds

Tondini di formaggio

THESE DELICIOUS DISCS of fried creamy cheese are irresistible. I read about these *cicchetti* in Mariù Salvatori de Zuliani's Venetian book and couldn't resist the sound of them: a sort of thick béchamel enriched with cheese and left to cool before cutting out rounds that are crumbed and fried. I have also tried making these in the oven and I can confirm they come out very, very well this way if you do not feel like frying – and I am always sceptical of baking things that should be fried. I like these served together with the artichoke bottoms (see page 62).

Makes approx. 20 cicchetti

1 tablespoon butter
1½ tablespoons plain (all-purpose) flour
250 ml (8½ fl oz/1 cup) full-cream (whole) milk
3 eggs
200 g (7 oz) provola cheese, or another good melting cheese, diced or shredded
80 g (2¾ oz) dry breadcrumbs
vegetable oil, for frying

In a small saucepan, melt the butter over a low heat. Add the flour and a splash of the milk and stir it in with a wooden spoon until you have a thick but smooth paste. Beat two of the eggs with the rest of the milk and slowly add this to the pot while stirring. Add the cheese and stir until it is all melted together and smooth. Pour onto a greased baking tray approximately 20 × 30 cm (8 in × 1 ft 12 in) in size (like something you might bake a lasagne in) and allow to cool.

Cut out small circles with a shot glass or cookie cutter – with any excess, you can melt it back together and keep cutting it out. Alternatively, simply cut into small squares, about 5 × 5 cm (2 × 2 in) and you will have exactly 24 squares ready for frying. In a small bowl, beat the last egg, and in another small, shallow bowl, place the breadcrumbs. Dip each cheese round first into the egg and then in breadcrumbs and place on a plate or tray until they are all crumbed.

Heat enough vegetable oil in a wide pan so that there is at least 1 cm (½ in) oil and fry over a medium heat on both sides until golden brown, about 2 minutes total.

If you choose to try baking this in the oven instead of frying, place the crumbed rounds of cheese on a baking tray lined with baking paper, drizzle with olive oil and bake at 190°C (375°F) for about 10 minutes, or until puffed and golden. Leftovers are also delicious reheated in the oven until melty.

Fried meatballs

Polpette di carne

THE DEEP-FRIED MEATBALLS AT Venice's Alla Vedova are legendary. I will never forget my first taste of them. It was December 2010. We were visiting my friend Rosa to celebrate her husband Massimo's birthday and the plan was to sustain ourselves entirely on *cicchetti* for the whole weekend.

There is something I find incredibly romantic about Venice in the winter. The short days, the threat of sloshing about in knee-high *acqua alta*, the damp, cold air and the festive season seem to create the perfect excuse for zipping into the nearest *bàcaro* for a quick *cicchetto* and a cheek-flushing glass of wine (although to be honest I could probably find a good excuse for *bàcaro*-hopping no matter what time of the year).

We started at Arco near the Rialto, the place where your first *cicchetto* in Venice should always be *baccalà mantecato* and Prosecco. Then we trudged over the wet stones to Piazza San Marco to treat ourselves to a spritz at Caffè Florian, which has been doing what it does since 1720. A drink at the mid-nineteenth century bar inside, standing at the counter, is surprisingly affordable considering that you pay an arm and a leg for a cappuccino if you happen to sit down at a table outside in the square. But the piazza on a wet winter evening is eerily empty; except for some solitary rose sellers and the smell of pigeons, it doesn't take much to imagine you are walking into an eighteenth-century version of Venice in moments like these.

Our last stop, finally, is Alla Vedova ('the Widow', as it is lovingly known, although technically its actual name is Trattoria Ca' d'Oro) and the journey here is for one thing and one thing only: *Polpette di carne* (see page 132). After our brisk walk cutting through the narrowest of *calli* to get to the Strada Nova, we crowd in through the front door and stand with the others at the marble bar waiting for freshly fried *polpette* while we are instantly handed an *ombra*, a little glass of wine, to keep us company. On display in the small wooden counter are also *sarde in saor* (see page 58) and crisp, deep-fried sardines with soft white polenta. But, finally, the *polpette* arrive – crunchy on the outside and impossibly soft and juicy inside – and then they keep flying fresh out of the kitchen so we keep eating them, and ordering more ombre. And so, a successful night of *cicchetti* concludes.

Thanks to these *polpette*, Alla Vedova is considered a culinary institution. Any cookbook that speaks of Venice offers a version inspired by the deep-brown, glowing *polpette* of Alla Vedova, which is supposedly a closely guarded secret. Every recipe I've seen is different. The main question is whether the *polpette* are made with fresh minced (ground) beef, which is probably the most convenient, or – more traditional – boiled leftover beef (or other 'bits'). The incredible softness that contrasts with the crunchy coating can be attributed to breadcrumbs in the filling, or perhaps soft white bread soaked in milk, and mashed potatoes. Or a combination. There is usually an egg, perhaps some cheese and, in many cases, mortadella or *salame* for flavour.

In *Venezia*, Tessa Kiros calls for fresh minced (ground) beef, floury potatoes, a couple of tablespoons of parmesan and a small egg to bind the filling together. Russell Norman is more generous with the eggs, and his filling of fresh mince includes breadcrumbs soaked in milk and 100 g (3½ oz/1 cup) grated parmesan.

Valeria Necchio, in *Veneto*, makes hers with boiled beef (or any leftover beef) and spiced *sopressa* (an aged Venetian *salame* with DOP status: the kind that you'll see in Jacopo da Bassano's painting of *Christ in the House of Martha, Mary and Lazarus* from 1577 at the Pitti Palace in Florence; while the main event is happening off to the side, the real show-stopper is the food in the kitchen: baskets of glistening fish, plucked poultry, carafes of red wine and an unmistakable *sopressa* being sliced). She softens them with white bread soaked in milk and mashed potato. I feel Necchio's recipe is very much like the most traditional Venetian recipes for *polpette*. Similarly, Sandro Brandolisio in his *cicchetti* book of the 1950s and 60s calls for leftover cooked meat. He adds ham, mortadella and *salame*, one boiled potato and a grating of nutmeg and Grana cheese.

Mariù Salvatori de Zuliani has a recipe for *polpette* using fresh mince, but she notes it is usually made with leftover meat so that it isn't thrown away and that, either way, the main scope of making *polpette di carne* is to give sustenance to children who are growing or for whoever is in need of a pick-me-up with something substantial. She adds nutmeg too, fries them in butter and serves them with radicchio di Treviso.

De Zuliani also includes three interesting recipes for sweet meatballs – recipes that she notes are no longer in use in Venice. Using leftover meat, one recipe includes sultanas, pine nuts and candied citron, along with a small glass of rum. Another is mixed with *luganega* (Venetian sausage), milk, parmesan, nutmeg, sultanas and pine nuts. As a final touch, these deep-fried *polpette* are sprinkled with sugar.

The other recipe, she notes, is from the 1800s and involves a filling of meat (fresh mince or already cooked beef), cinnamon, parsley and an egg. It's fried in lard to get a good crust, then finished slowly in butter and served in a sweet zabaione – a spoonful of sugar, an egg yolk and rum cooked over a medium–high heat until fluffy and creamy.

Interestingly, in *La Cucina di Venezia e della Laguna* (2016), by Maria Teresa Di Marco and Marie Cécille Ferré, the recipe is for fresh minced (ground) veal, mortadella and mashed potatoes and two spoons of parmesan – according to Alla Vedova's cook, Ada's, 'secret' recipe, they say. Hold on. I thought this was a *secret* recipe.

After digging around for Ada's 'secret' recipe, I found a Facebook group called *Veneziani a Tavola* ('Venetians at the Table') with a post entitled, 'The mystery of the polpette of Alla Vedova', claiming that after decades of creating the *polpette* that no Venetian can pass up, the cook, Ada, has finally shared her recipe from her archives: 'Some slices of mortadella, a couple of potatoes, boiled and passed through a mouli, mixed with 300 g (10½ oz) minced meat, grated Grana cheese, two eggs, parsley and garlic, salt and pepper, and a little bit of breadcrumbs to adjust the consistency. Make balls with your hands, a light crumbing, and fry in abundant boiling oil.' The debate continues in the comments, however, as to whether or not it is indeed the real recipe. Personally, I think the best way to enjoy Alla Vedova's *polpette* is at Alla Vedova. But making these and enjoying them piping hot as they come out of the frying pan comes a close second.

Makes 24 polpette

1 potato
1–2 slices white bread, crusts removed
60 ml (2 fl oz/¼ cup) full-cream
  (whole) milk
100 g (3½ oz) mortadella
1 garlic clove, peeled
a few parsley sprigs
450 g (1 lb) minced (ground) beef
1 egg
2 tablespoons grated parmesan
½ teaspoon salt, or to taste, plus extra
  to serve
50 g (1¾ oz/½ cup) dry breadcrumbs
vegetable oil, for frying

Boil the potato until a fork easily goes through it, then peel and mash. Set aside in a large bowl.

In a separate bowl, soak the bread in the milk for a few minutes, then squeeze the excess milk out and add the bread to the mashed potato.

In a food processor, or finely chopping by hand, mince the mortadella, garlic and parsley together. Place in a large bowl with the mashed potato.

Add the beef, egg and parmesan and season with salt and pepper. Mix everything well with your hands, then roll into golf ball–sized balls and set them on a tray until they are all shaped. In a shallow bowl, add the breadcrumbs then roll the meatballs through the breadcrumbs to coat lightly but entirely.

In a frying pan, pour enough oil to cover a layer of meatballs, about 4–5 cm (1½–2 in). Heat over a medium heat until it reaches 170°C (340°F) and, when the oil is visibly shimmering and the end of a wooden spoon dipped in it is immediately surrounded by tiny bubbles, drop in the meatballs (you should do it in batches, filling the pan only halfway each batch) and cook until deep brown all over, about 4–5 minutes. Drain on kitchen paper and sprinkle immediately with salt to taste.

Cod fritters

Polpette di baccalà

THIS IS AN IRRESISTIBLE WAY TO enjoy _baccalà_, and it is a favourite in my family, where we also do this with other preserved fish such as tinned tuna. You could use pre-soaked dried stockfish or salt cod _baccalà_ for this, just be aware of adjusting for salt for the latter even after soaking (speaking of which, you should always try a little taste after soaking salt cod to ensure it has been adequately desalted). You could even consider making this with leftover _Baccalà mantecato_ (page 46), or indeed any leftover white fish.

Makes approx. 12 cicchetti

500 g (1 lb 2 oz) baccalà, already soaked
1 garlic clove, whole but peeled
50 g (1¾ oz) (about 3 slices) stale white bread, crusts removed
60–125 ml (2–4 fl oz/¼–½ cup) full-cream (whole) milk
1 egg
40 g (1½ oz) dry breadcrumbs
vegetable oil, for frying

NOTE If you're using bread that isn't quite stale yet you won't need as much milk. For instructions on how to desalt and prepare salt cod, if it isn't already soaked (and you should _always_ double check), see the note on _Baccalà fritto_, page 136.

Place the pre-soaked baccalà and garlic in a pot of boiling water and poach for about 15 minutes.

In the meantime, soak the stale bread in the milk (the amount will depend on how stale the bread is), about 10–15 minutes.

When the baccalà is ready, remove any large bones or skin, then mash by hand or blend in a food processor with the garlic clove, along with the bread, squeezed of any excess milk, the egg and add freshly ground pepper and a good pinch of salt (if using dried, unsalted stockfish or salted baccalà, you may not need much – I usually take a little taste to be sure here). Roll the mixture into small balls or cylinders like croquettes and then roll in the breadcrumbs to lightly but entirely coat them.

Heat enough vegetable oil in a frying pan so that there is at least 2 cm (¾ in) oil and heat over a medium heat. Fry the polpette on all sides until golden brown, about 2 minutes total. Drain on absorbent kitchen paper and serve.

Baccalà fritto

DELICIOUS MORSELS OF BATTERED,
deep-fried cod are a classic street food,
and one that has a particular following
where there are also important Jewish
communities in Italy, for example in
Rome's and in Venice's Jewish quarters.
In Tuscan-born Edda Servi's wonderful
cookbook *The Classic Cuisine of the
Italian Jews* (1981), she has a recipe
for what she calls *pezzetti*, which are
finger-shaped pieces of salt cod dipped
in a flour and water batter, fried and
served with lemon wedges. Venetian
gastronome Sandro Brandolisio in his
book on *cicchetti* from the 1950s and
60s says he likes to use milk instead of
water for the batter, an egg and flour,
similar to the batter here. But some
only dust them in flour before frying.
Other Venetian recipes call for poaching
the cod first in milk (then use the milk
for the batter), which also helps the
de-salting process.

Makes 16 pieces

1 × 500 g (1 lb 2 oz) fillet baccalà (salt
    cod), pre-soaked
1 egg, separated
80 ml (2½ fl oz/⅓ cup) well-chilled
    full-cream (whole) milk
75 g (2¾ oz/½ cup) plain (all-purpose)
    flour, plus extra for dusting
vegetable oil, for frying

Pull the skin off the salt cod fillet (it is
easiest to do this from the wide end,
rather than the tail end) and pick out any
large bones that may be remaining – there
are usually a few, so a feel with your hands
to find them and a pair of sturdy tweezers
is best for this. Make sure that the fish is
as dry as possible. Slice the fish into 16 or
so bite-sized pieces, ideally no thicker than
your thumb. Dust in flour and set aside.

To make the batter, beat the egg white
with a pinch of salt until it is fluffy and
foamy. In another bowl, whisk together
the yolk and the milk and then add the
flour, until you have a smooth batter. Fold
in the egg whites gently, then submerge
the pieces of salt cod into the batter.

Heat a pan with enough vegetable oil to
cover the pieces of fish (about 3 cm/1¼ in)
over a medium heat. The oil will start to
look like it is shimmering and the end
of a wooden spoon dipped into the oil
will be surrounded by tiny bubbles. Fry
just a couple pieces at a time to avoid
overcrowding the pan until they are golden
brown and crisp, about 4–6 minutes total.
You want these to fry quite slowly so that
the fish cooks through, but if you find they
are browning much quicker than that time
takes, the oil is getting too hot. You can
turn it down a notch and you can also add
some cold oil to the pan to adjust the heat.
Drain on kitchen paper and immediately
sprinkle with salt, if it needs it.

NOTE This recipe uses salt cod rather than dried stockfish because it is fleshier (you could do this too with fresh cod fillets if that is easier for you to find). With salt cod, you will need to start this recipe at least 2 days before you want to use it, unless you have access to pre-soaked salt cod that has already been through the soaking and desalting process. It's much easier to do at home than when using dried stockfish, thankfully. Simply rinse off the excess salt and place the fish in a bowl of fresh water and set in the fridge. Change the water every 8 hours – or if you don't remember the exact number of hours, just remember to fill up with fresh water five times in 48 hours. Have a little taste at this point – if you are squeamish about tasting it raw, just pinch off a piece and quickly boil it then taste. The important thing is to check that it isn't too salty, as all your efforts will be ruined with a too-salty-to-eat fish. If too salty, place back in the water for a further 12–24 hours. Note that the tail end of thinner pieces will be saltier than thicker parts of the fish. Drain, pat dry and you can begin the recipe. Alternatively, you could do what American chef Renee Erickson does, which is what she calls 'home-made salt cod': fresh cod fillets, trimmed into pieces and sandwiched between salt to cover entirely, more or less the same weight as the fish, and left to firm up in the fridge for 4 hours before using (here, too, I would check for salt, but do it the opposite way: rinse off the salt, pat dry and taste-test it about 3 hours in – if it is firm and suitably salted, then it is ready, otherwise leave it an extra hour. Note that thinner pieces of fish will salt quicker than thicker pieces).

Fried soft-shell lagoon crabs Moeche fritte

WE SPENT A FOGGY WEEKEND in autumn searching for *moeche*: soft-shelled green lagoon crabs that change their coats for a fleeting moment, a matter of hours, every autumn and spring. I wasn't even sure it would be possible to find what I had come looking for, but we booked a hotel on the Giudecca – that long, thin island that lies under the belly of Venice's fish (have you ever noticed it looks like a fish from above?) – and we waited for news from a friend of a friend who knew someone. Not just anyone, but the so-called 'last of the *moecanti*', the last family of fishermen in Venice who have farmed and harvested lagoon crabs for centuries on the Giudecca.

I was pinching myself as Manuel Bognolo pulled up to pick us up on Denis, his *bragozzo*, or boat, right around the corner from the hotel, an ex-flour mill, where Manuel used to play with his friends as a boy. He took us through the canals and around the rarely seen underside of the Giudecca to the shack – unreachable by foot – where his brothers picked through the crabs, which were slowly sliding or crawling sideways on a slightly inclined wooden board into a large bucket to be tipped back into the sea. To me, they all looked the same, but the *moecanti* could spot the *moeche* in an instant just by the shade of their bellies. It took only a glance and the crab was swept up quickly and placed into a small bucket.

What followed will remain etched in my memory as possibly the best day of my life. Manuel took a bowl full of *moeche* right from the shack, stepped back onto the boat where he had set up an enviably well-equipped makeshift kitchen and he fried them.

A recipe popular in Venetian restaurants and books describes placing the crabs in a bowl full of beaten eggs and waiting for them to greedily eat it all before frying them, but Manuel insists that's not the real way to prepare this Venetian specialty. His suspicion is that this is a tradition from the *terraferma*, the mainland, as a way to stretch the meal and fill you up, countering the need to buy more crabs (which have their price, about 80 euro a kilo). And besides, Manuel added, eggs are more plentiful in the countryside than they are in the lagoon. It's certainly not the way fishermen would make it. I was convinced. Manuel took about 100 g (3½ oz) *moeche* per person and dusted them lightly but completely in flour. Then he fried them in plenty of vegetable oil at 175°C (345°F) until the shells changed colour from lagoon green to deep red. And that was it.

He opened a bottle of Ribolla Gialla and we talked while we ate and sipped, floating on the foggy lagoon, about his family, their history, climate change, how things have changed in Venice. In the 1990s they could bring in 10–12,000 kg (22–26,500 lb) of crabs in one day. This particular day that we were together they found 3 kg (6 lb 10 oz), but, I'm told, spring is usually a better season. Manuel talked with romance about the cycle of the *moeche*, the male crabs, who change their shells twice a year, in spring and autumn, as they grow. The female, *la masanetta*, undergoes the same shell change in the summer and this is when the *moecanti* fishermen stay away, as it's mating season. Manuel described the way the male crab, after mating, tucks the soft-shell female under one leg to protect her until her shell grows back as the same way the lion of San Marco – the symbol of Venice – is holding his book.

I've never tasted anything like these *moeche*, but there is another secret that Manuel let me in on: he has served us a specialty normally set aside for the fishermen themselves, what they call *strapasae* or, in Italian, *stroppiciate* – the *moeche* that are the softest but that don't make it to restaurants who ask for the prettiest-looking, pristine ones. *Strapasae*, even though they are full of water, are much more delicious and the fishermen get to take them home. We finished the last delightful, crunchy bites and the final drops of our glasses and glided back over the water at sunset, and I couldn't help but think the taste of these *moeche* were pure Venice.

Fried Venetian prawns

Schie fritte

THIS DISH IS ALSO KNOWN SIMPLY as *polenta e schie*, indicating how important it is that these prawns, tiny grey shrimp that are fished out of the Venetian lagoon, are served together with polenta. There is something really satisfying about this contrast of textures: the soft, velvety bed of polenta topped with the incredibly crunchy prawns, which are eaten – strictly – heads, shells and all. No Venetian would bother to sit and peel these tiny prawns one by one, it would be unthinkable. But also, you'd really miss that crunch, which is vital to the whole experience of eating *schie*.

Note that this is traditionally eaten with white polenta, which is a soft, floppy style of polenta, but you could also eat these *schie* just as they are as a delicious crunchy snack, like chips, perfect for aperitivo. This amount would easily serve at least four people as part of a meal, but if serving smaller plates as *cicchetti*, you could stretch it to eight.

Serves 6–8 as antipasto or cicchetti

500 g (1 lb 2 oz) live, very small prawns (shrimp) (school prawns or brown shrimp)
1½ tablespoons plain (all-purpose) flour, for dusting
vegetable oil, for frying (see page 118 for frying notes)
creamy white polenta or polenta crostini (see page 50), to serve

Place the whole prawns in a large bowl and dust with the flour, mixing gently so they are all covered lightly. Pour the vegetable oil into a wide frying pan with at least 2 cm (¾ in) oil and heat over a medium heat to 180°C (350°F).

Fry the prawns in a few batches – they should only take about 30 seconds to cook (they will turn orange and the flour will become crisp and golden). Drain on absorbent kitchen paper and sprinkle generously with salt. When they are all ready, serve them with hot, creamy white polenta, or with grilled white polenta crostini.

NOTE You need really tiny prawns (shrimp) for this that can be bought live, ideally, or are extremely fresh, as they are eaten whole. A very close substitute for *schie* would be school prawns in Australia, which are equally small, wild-caught prawns often found in estuaries, or brown shrimp in the US or UK (where it is also known as Morcombe Bay shrimp, which you can often find already peeled; go for the whole ones). Do not use already cooked or peeled prawns for this.

Crumbed zucchini

Zucchine impanate

I LIKE TO MAKE THESE with round zucchini (courgette), but you could use regular long ones and do long strips instead, or you could also use eggplant (aubergine). These are delicious as they are but try also using them as a base for topping with a soft cheese such as buffalo mozzarella or stracchino, perhaps with a fresh mint or basil leaf as a garnish. These are lovely warm or at room temperature but best on the day they are made as they tend to go soggy if left overnight.

Makes 10–12 cicchetti

400 g (14 oz) zucchini (courgette) (about 2 large round ones)
1½ tablespoons plain (all-purpose) flour
1 egg, beaten
70 g (2½ oz) dry breadcrumbs
vegetable oil, for frying

Slice the zucchini into thick discs, about 0.5–1 cm (¼–½ in) thick. Get three shallow bowls ready: one with the flour, one with the egg and the other with breadcrumbs. Add a pinch of salt to the beaten egg. Dip both sides of the zucchini discs into the flour, then into the egg to cover and, finally, in the breadcrumbs to coat entirely.

Heat enough vegetable oil in a frying pan so that there is at least 1 cm (½ in) oil and heat over a medium heat to around 180°C (350°F). Fry both sides until deep golden brown, about 1½ minutes total. Drain momentarily on absorbent kitchen paper, then sprinkle with salt and serve.

Dawn at the fish market in Burano

Piatti
Piccoli
Piatti
Piccoli

Piatti piccoli
Small plates

Insalata di mare
Seafood salad

Insalata di aringa grigliata
Grilled smoked herring salad

Insalata di Gallina Padovana
Padova chicken salad

Asparagi con salsa d'uova
Asparagus with egg yolk sauce

Canestrelli gratinati coi funghi
Gratin scallops with mushrooms

Funghi e polenta
Mushrooms and polenta

Seppie al nero
Cuttlefish stewed in its ink

Ton fresco in tecia
Fresh tuna stewed with tomatoes

Baccalà al pomodoro
Salt cod stewed in tomatoes

Carpaccio alla Cipriani
Cipriani's carpaccio

Fegato alla veneziana
Venetian-style liver

Patate alla veneziana
Venetian-style potatoes

Frittata dei frati
Friar's wild herb frittata

— *Elizabeth David, from* Italian Food

'In other markets, on other shores, the unfamiliar fishes may be vivid, mysterious, repellent, fascinating and bright with splendid colour; only in Venice do they look good enough to eat. In Venice even ordinary dole and ugly great skate are striped with delicate lilac lights, the sardines shine like newly-minted silver coins, pink Venetian scampi are fat and fresh, infinitely enticing in the early dawn.'

Right
The Rialto market

The seasons of the Rialto market

When I'm in Venice, the first place I'm drawn to is the market. It's a spectacle on its own; there is always something to see and a constant flow of people – or seafood or birds – to watch.

You can spot the season, if you know the clues, just by looking at the abundant fish, displayed on huge beds of ice and looking like live Dutch still-life paintings, often moving, being spied on by oversized seagulls that wait for the fishmongers to turn their backs for a moment to steal a sardine. There are enormous piles of whole cuttlefish, smudged by their own ink, that are at their best in spring and autumn and disappear very quickly from the counters, and shellfish of all kinds – snails, queen scallops, mussels, clams (vongole) and tightly tied bags of long cappelunghe, razor clams, if it isn't their mating period between April and May. There might be an enormous whole tuna waiting to be carved, gleaming sea bass and striped mackerel, tiny whole squid, piovra, large whole octopus, and moscardini, their smaller cousins, and always the long, stiff grey tails of dried stockfish sticking out of vessels. The freshest, plump scampi. Wriggling mantis shrimp and lobsters that might walk right off their perch. In the winter and spring, too, you can find the best examples of granceola, spider crab. Latti di seppia is another specialty, one that you might only find in Venice – cuttlefish ovaries, which are boiled briefly and dressed with olive oil, parsley and pepper and eaten as cicchetti, ideally with a glass of chilled Prosecco.

It's the place to know what is in season. Venice has a unique lagoon environment and a strong link to the comings and goings of the seasons. Venetian specialties are truly fleeting – the moeche (soft-shell crabs) available for a couple of months in the spring and autumn change their shells in a matter of hours. And the special tiny castraure artichokes have a season of 10, maybe 15 days in spring. Whenever I visit Venice, I have this urgency to enjoy that special thing that is only in season for that moment.

Elizabeth David has a wonderful account in An Omelette and a Glass of Wine (1984) that describes this seasonal urgency on a visit to Locanda Cipriani on the island of Torcello in May of 1969, where she was introduced to risotto with bruscandoli, wild hop shoots, a wild green found locally only in the first 10 days of May. The next day, at Romano's on Burano island, she had it again and was told that she might even find some at the Rialto market, 'Hurry though. The season ends any day now.' So she went back to Torcello to have her fill again and later at the Rialto market found an old woman selling a few bunches of it: 'it's the last of the year, she said – took it back to my hotel, stuck it in a glass so that I could make a drawing of it. When I came back in the evening the zealous chambermaid had thrown it away. No, next morning there was no old lady selling bruscandoli in the market. For once it was true, that warning "tomorrow it will be finished".' After reading this, I went looking for it on my next visit to Venice's Rialto market. It was the 1st May, but 52 years after Elizabeth David's encounter with bruscandoli. And there they were in piles between the plump stalks of Bassano white asparagus and the castraure, wrapped in bunches in pink satin ribbon, as you would only see in a Venetian market.

Venice's lagoon produce

Venice's cuisine is one that is, substantially, very simple and, while the 'magpie' city loved collecting things, including ingredients, from other cultures, there was an abundance of local products too.

Without a doubt, 'Fish is the most important element of Venetian cooking', as Ada Boni writes in *Italian Regional Cooking*. Built on the water, Venice is blessed with a bounty of seafood; even the most ancient of testimonies describe the array of fish found and the ways they were prepared in the lagoon – usually very simply grilled for larger fish, or fried for small fish, and if not eaten right away, perhaps marinated *in saor* (see page 58). On the island of Murano, eel, skinned and scored, was prepared in a nest of bay leaves and cooked near the embers of the roaring ovens used to heat and melt glass. Indeed, many of the most special seafood dishes today are the ones that were once considered 'poor': sardines, fried and marinated *in saor*, *moeche* (soft-shell crabs, see page 138) and *schie*, the tiny grey prawns (shrimp, see page 140), both fished out of the lagoon and eaten whole, fried and on a gleaming puddle of white polenta. One of the classic symbols of Venetian seafood today is also one of the most impressive-looking, *granceola*, or spider crab, where the meat of the boiled live crab (those in the know will use both the male crab for sweeter meat and a female crab for more abundant meat, together) is almost always served inside an upturned shell as a bowl, dressed very simply with olive oil, lemon and parsley.

Meat was – and still is – secondary to the seafood. If it isn't obvious enough, there was nowhere for large animals to graze on an island city built on a lagoon, though live cattle was imported from the East and there was a slaughterhouse for fresh meat on the Lido (offal, in particular liver and tripe, were and still are popular – such as in the classic Venetian-style liver with onions, page 174). Otherwise, beef was usually prepared in ways that used the meat of old animals that could no longer work. Even horse was traditionally eaten for the same reason – those too tired for the return journey back to Genova were usually slaughtered in Venice, writes Riley, and often made into bresaola.

There is also a revered, very traditional dish of preserved mutton known as *castradina*, where salted and smoked mutton imported from Albania or Dalmatia (a historical region of Croatia, along the east shore of the Adriatic Sea) is cooked with cabbage, onion, bay leaf, juniper berries and wine or stock into a stew. It's a traditional dish prepared for the *Madonna della Salute*, 'Our Lady of Health', celebrating the end of the devastating 1630 Plague every 21st November with the beautiful Basilica built on the Punta della Dogana that you can see from Piazza San Marco. It is a dish that Mariù Salvatori de Zuliani writes was 'obligatory on the tables of the poor, the nobility and merchants, alike'. This mutton (or any leftovers) were also used to prepare *riso in cavroman*, where you can also find a Levantine influence: a stew of tomatoes and mutton, with a soffritto of celery, onion and carrot, spiced with cinnamon, nutmeg and cloves, finished with a handful of rice per person.

Above
Wild hop shoots at the
Rialto market

Left
A bag of *moeche*
(soft-shell crabs)

Piatti piccoli

While researching the many traditional recipes over centuries of Venetian cooking, I noticed that fresh pork is a real rarity in Venice, presumably because of the difficulty of keeping pigs, as with beef. You do, however, find the odd recipe for pig's trotters, boiled then cooked with lardo, onion and cabbage, or liver, cooked in the same way as veal liver, but you mostly see pork in the form of sausages and *salame*, the most traditional of which are *luganega* and *sopressa,* respectively, preparations that make good use of all parts of the pig and spices.

Poultry was a far more important ingredient in Venetian kitchens. Chickens, turkeys, pigeons and geese (an important part of Venetian-Jewish cuisine), birds known as *da cortile*, could be easily kept in the small courtyards attached to *palazzi*. Turkey cooked with pomegranate juice (a Persian-sounding dish) is traditional, while roast duck is a special and festive dish for the Festa del Redentore that Venetians celebrate in July for the end of the Plague that gripped the city in the sixteenth century. As important as seafood was the hunting of wild water birds attracted to the lagoon as well – Vittore Carpaccio's painting of a bird hunt on the lagoon from 1490 shows how it was done with a bow and arrow while standing on a gondola (although there is an argument as to whether these birds were eaten or hunted for their feathers). *Gallina Padovana* (see page 158) was particularly appreciated for its meat, an ancient breed with a prominent crest, which is clearly depicted in Jacopo da Verona's 1397 fresco of the Annunciation in Padova. There is a legend that during the thirteenth century a treaty was drawn between Padova and Venice that forced the Paduans to bring thirty of their indigenous hens to Venice each year, an accord that lasted five centuries.

The saline soils of the islands around Venice provided a place for vegetables to grow successfully and, even today, much of Venice's local produce comes from the island of Sant'Erasmo – artichokes, especially the best-known young *castraure* (see page 64), which are picked off the plant early, but also wild hop shoots, peas, zucchini (courgette), beans, eggplant (aubergine), pumpkin and radicchio, the latter of which is from nearby Chioggia and Treviso (see page 61). Even local grapes, some of which are being revived by the Michelin-starred restaurant Venissa, on the island of Mazzorbo (see page 87).

Like the seafood, vegetables are cooked very simply. The preferred way is *in tecia*, dialect for 'in the pot', with a bit of olive oil, garlic and herbs. In fact, you will find that this simple combination of garlic and parsley, minced very finely, with olive oil is the favourite way to accompany fish or vegetables – and, mostly, not much else is needed. When in doubt, and when you have absolutely gleamingly fresh seafood and seasonal vegetables as they do in Venice, the only thing you need to do to reproduce it in a Venetian way is use these three key ingredients.

Olive oil was imported into Venice from their colonies on the Greek islands and sold to Lombardy, Trentino and Bavaria. Because of its availability to the Venetians (who kept 40 per cent of what they imported for their own use) olive oil was (and still is) the preferred fat for cooking. It's interesting to note too, that for preparations such as *sarde in saor* (and the many variations; see page 58), which have roots in Venice's Jewish quarter, it was preferred to use olive oil for frying (which was often prepared on a Friday for Shabbat, the Jewish day of rest), rather than animal fat so that the next day the fat did not solidify and there was no further cooking required.

Piatti piccoli

Seafood salad

Insalata di mare

THIS IS A CLASSIC SEAFOOD recipe that is much loved all along the Italian coast. It is popular served along with *cicchetti* as it's a good one to prepare in advance and keeps well chilled in the fridge. I like to keep the mussels in their shells and eat them right out of their shells with my hands. My husband, Marco, prefers not having to fiddle with them and always wants to remove their shells before serving them. We compromise by doing both.

Serves 4

150 g (5½ oz) cherry tomatoes
80 ml (2½ fl oz/⅓ cup) olive oil, plus
    extra for drizzling
150 g (5½ oz) calamari (about 1 medium-
    sized one)
500 g (1 lb 2 oz) mussels
1 potato, peeled and diced
150 g (5½ oz) prawns (shrimp) (about 12)
½ celery stalk, preferably the top half
    with leaves still attached
handful of parsley leaves
1 garlic clove
juice of 1 lemon

VARIATIONS You can use any favourite seafood here, and you could even just use one type – how about just prawns (shrimp), for example? This is a combination I particularly like, but here are some other ideas you could consider: octopus instead of the calamari; vongole or other clams instead of the mussels; crab meat; tinned or fresh tuna, salmon or mackerel, gently poached. You can also keep it strictly seafood and remove the vegetables, if you wish, or add even more vegetables – I also like black olives, thinly sliced fennel or marinated artichokes here.

Halve the cherry tomatoes and drizzle over some olive oil and a pinch of salt and let them marinate in a bowl while you prepare the other ingredients.

Clean the calamari (see page 122) and scrub the mussels with a metal scourer – pull the beards from the mussels if they haven't already been cleaned by the fishmonger (if you are buying them vacuum-packed they are usually already cleaned).

Place the potato in a pot of cold water and cook until tender, about 15 minutes. Use a slotted spoon to fish out the potato pieces and set them aside to cool, then add them to the tomatoes. Keep the water in the pot boiling for cooking the seafood.

Poach the calamari for 1–1½ minutes and remove with a slotted spoon, setting aside with the potato.

Poach the prawns whole for 1 minute and drain, then add them to the calamari.

In a separate pan, place the mussels over a medium heat and steam them open. Give the pan a shake to make sure any underneath have the chance to open. It should take about 2 minutes. Remove some of their shells if you like and add the mussels to the rest of the seafood along with the celery and its leaves.

Make a dressing by finely mincing the parsley, garlic and a pinch of salt together on a chopping board. Place in a bowl and whisk in the lemon juice and olive oil, along with some freshly ground pepper. Toss together with the salad ingredients and serve. This is quite nice when it has had a little bit of time for the flavours to mingle, for example, prepared in the morning for lunch.

Piatti piccoli

Grilled smoked herring salad

Insalata di aringa grigliata

THIS SALAD IS PARTLY inspired by a recipe in the Veneto chapter of Ada Boni's _Italian Regional Cooking_. It utilises _renga_, as it is known in the Veneto, or _aringa_, smoked whole herring, which is another preserved fish like _baccalà_ and _stoccafisso_ that comes from a northern European tradition but is well used in this corner of Italy. You might find it as a sandwich filling (use it in place of tinned mackerel or tuna, for example); Cantinone già Schiavi offer a _cicchetto_ with herring and _scarola_, bitter curly endive (salty and bitter are so good together), and it works really well as a simple topping on a slice of polenta with the classic parsley, garlic, lemon and olive oil.

The herrings are first salt-preserved and then cold-smoked, and the time that they are smoked (and therefore their quality and flavour) can differ greatly. They usually come in two different qualities, noted in Italian as _dorata_, golden, the most prestigious and the most flavourful, which is smoked for 3 days, or _argentata_, silver, which is a bit more delicate as it is only smoked for a maximum of 12 hours. Sometimes smoked herring can be eaten just as it is, while others need to go through a process of desalting – usually soaking for 24 hours in milk – in order to make them palatable. That said, my mother-in-law's grandfather used to take the salty smoked herring as is and rub it against thick slices of polenta, to _insaporire_, for extra flavour.

Ada Boni uses the herring as it comes – in other words, not cooked or even desalted, in a salad with onion, white beans, black olives and boiled eggs. But I have to admit that once I discovered a method from Pellegrino Artusi's 1891 cookbook _Scienza in Cucina e l'Arte di Mangiar Bene_ that he describes as _aringa ingentilita_, 'refined herring', it quickly became my favourite way to eat smoked herring. He first calls for desalting in boiling hot milk for 8–10 hours, then grilling it and dressing in olive oil and lemon juice. It's absolutely delicious. He describes also placing the herring in cold water and bringing to the boil, poaching for 3 minutes, then rinsing in cold water again before eating as another method to 'refine' it, which you could too if you prefer.

Serves 4 as a shared cicchetto or antipasto

1 smoked herring
125 ml (4 fl oz/½ cup) hot full-cream (whole) milk
½ red onion, thinly sliced
3–4 radicchio leaves, torn
1 celery stalk with leaves, thinly sliced
60 g (2 oz) cooked borlotti (cranberry) beans
1 hard-boiled egg (see page 77), quartered
¼ green apple, skin on, finely sliced
a few parsley sprigs, finely chopped
2 tablespoons extra-virgin olive oil
1 tablespoon red-wine vinegar, or lemon juice, plus extra for the onions if desired

Place the herring in a container with a lid and pour the hot milk over it. Leave to cool, then place in the fridge for 8 hours and then drain of the milk and rinse in fresh water. Pat completely dry. To obtain the fillets, cut the head of the fish off, and then, using the backbone as a guide, slice lengthways just above the backbone and as close to the bones as possible. Remove the backbone and any large bones that may be remaining, any guts, and cut off the tail. You should now have two clean fillets.

Grill the fillets of herring in a griddle pan over a high heat for 2 minutes, then let cool and break apart with your hands.

In the meantime, if you want to take the edge off the red onion, soak the slices in a bowl of hot water with a splash of red-wine vinegar while you prepare the salad. You can also choose to leave them as is; the bite goes quite nicely with the herring.

Arrange the salad with radicchio, celery, borlotti, the egg quarters, apple and the (drained) onion slices. Scatter over the herring and parsley and dress with the extra-virgin olive oil and vinegar. You probably won't need salt on this salad, but adjust to your taste.

Padova chicken salad

Insalata di Gallina Padovana

THIS RECIPE IS INSPIRED by a salad that is also known as *Insalata Gonzaga*, found in the cookbook by Bartolomeo Stefani, the chef of the House of Gonzaga in Mantua, *L'Arte di Ben Cucinare* from 1662, and is still a much-loved dish in the area (Mantua or Mantova is on the border of the Veneto in Lombardy). Traditionally made with *galletto*, a young chicken similar to a poussin, or with *cappone*, a castrated rooster, it is poached, then the meat is shredded and dressed simply with lemon zest, olive oil and vinegar, and an important, very specific pop of sweetness from sultanas. In the original seventeenth-century recipe, candied citron featured too, along with the feet of the chicken.

But getting closer to Venice, I was intrigued by a recipe in the Slow Food–produced cookbook *Ricette di Osterie del Veneto* for a similar recipe using *Gallina Padovana*, an ancient, Venetian heirloom breed of chicken with an impressive plume of feathers on its head, and the same *agrodolce*, or sweet-and-sour, flavours found in the Gonzaga salad (indeed familiar in many *in saor* dishes too). The recipe, proposed by Enoteca Angelo Rasi in Padova, includes salad leaves, green beans, beetroot (beets), sultanas, candied citron (or green apple), redcurrants and balsamic vinegar.

NOTE Try to get a really good chicken for this – organic and free-range – as it is so simply prepared. It will make a difference. If you are using a poussin then you can use the whole thing, otherwise I have suggested half a regular chicken. The chicken broth left over from cooking is wonderful for making soup with or for boiling and serving tortellini in, so save it for another use (it freezes well too). If you happen to have mostarda, that very spicy, nose-tingling fruit compote, you can use it in place of the mustard and honey in the dressing. Pomegranate seeds would be very fitting here too, if you have them – the juice or seeds of pomegranate are found in some ancient Venetian recipes such as *paeta*, roast turkey with pomegranate, butter and sage, very reminiscent of its Middle Eastern influence and the Persian dish *fesenjān* – their sweet-and-sour flavour goes really well here.

Serves 4 as antipasto

½ whole chicken
1 small onion
1 carrot
½ celery stalk
1–2 tablespoons sultanas
50 g (1¾ oz/1 cup) baby spinach, or
    other small salad leaf such as rocket
    (arugula)
1–2 tablespoons pine nuts
zest and juice of 1 lemon
2 tablespoons extra-virgin olive oil
1 teaspoon wholegrain mustard
1 teaspoon honey

To poach the chicken, place in a stockpot with the onion, carrot and celery and cover with cold water. Bring to a simmer and cook, covered, for 1–1½ hours, then turn off the heat but allow the chicken to cool in the stock. Pull the meat off the bone, shredded with either your hands or by chopping finely with a knife, and set aside. Keep the stock for another use.

Soak the sultanas in a glass of water (some like to use white wine) for about 20 minutes, then drain.

Arrange the salad leaves, shredded poached chicken, sultanas and pine nuts in a serving bowl.

For the dressing, whisk together the lemon zest and juice, olive oil, mustard and honey. Add a pinch of salt and some freshly ground pepper to taste, then dress the salad. You may not need all the dressing.

Piatti piccoli

Asparagus with egg yolk sauce

Asparagi con salsa d'uova

THIS IS A VERY CLASSIC approach to serving asparagus in the prime of the season. Asparagus is a wonderful Venetian vegetable, though white asparagus is particularly loved in this region. Nearby Bassano del Grappa is famous for their DOP (Protected Designation of Origin) status white asparagus and in the spring these plump, creamy white vegetables appear in the markets. There is just one local green variety of asparagus, Montine asparagus, that has been grown on the lagoon north of Venice for centuries, around the islands of Lio Piccolo, Mesole and Treporti, and is usually boiled or cooked in risotto.

This sauce is like a light mayonnaise, but simpler in a way as you really just throw everything into a blender. I like this just the way it is, but I'm also inclined to slink an anchovy or two over this too, or, if you're keeping this vegetarian, a spoonful of chopped capers.

Serves 6 as a starter, antipasto or side dish

2 eggs
bunch of asparagus
2 tablespoons lemon juice
2 tablespoons olive oil

Place the eggs in a small saucepan of boiling water and cook at a rapid simmer for 9 minutes for a hard-set yolk. Remove from the heat, drain the eggs and place in a bowl of cold water. When cool enough to handle, crack the egg all over, refresh the bowl of water and, with your hands in the water, begin to peel the eggs. The shell should come off very easily this way. You only need the yolks for this recipe, so save the whites for another recipe or do what I do – eat them as the cook's snack!

Trim the woody stems off the asparagus, then boil for about 10–15 minutes with a good pinch of salt depending on how thick they are, until tender. Rinse under cold water to stop them cooking further and set aside to drain.

In a small food processor or with a hand blender, or simply by hand, mash the egg yolks with the lemon juice and olive oil to a smooth, creamy sauce. Adjust to taste with salt and pepper. Serve the boiled asparagus with the sauce drizzled over the top.

Piatti piccoli

Gratin scallops with mushrooms

Canestrelli gratinati coi funghi

SCALLOPS SERVED in some kind of gratin is a classic, and these are perfect to serve as *cicchetti* – I mean, they even come with their own plates! This combination of mushroom and scallop is heavenly, and it is always received with much oohing and ahhing. Much like the squid with peas, where seafood is paired with a vegetable, there is some kind of magic that happens to the flavours – where here, the mushrooms soak up the liquid like sponges.

Makes 10 cicchetti

10 scallops
1–2 tablespoons olive oil
80 g (2¾ oz/4 tablespoons) butter
2 tablespoons plain (all-purpose) flour
250 ml (8½ fl oz/1 cup) full-cream (whole) milk
150 g (5½ oz/1⅔ cup) mushrooms (see Variations)
juice of 1 lemon
a few sprigs of parsley leaves, finely chopped
15 g (½ oz/5 teaspoons) dry breadcrumbs

VARIATIONS I use *chiodini* (honey fungus), but regular button mushrooms work well too. You could also leave out the mushrooms and simply cook these with the scallops and béchamel.

Clean the scallops, cut them off the shell if needed (reserving the shells), give them a quick rinse and pat dry. Sear them in a very hot pan with the oil for 1 minute on each side, or until they develop a golden-brown crust but are still bouncy and tender. Chop them roughly and set aside.

Make a béchamel by melting half of the butter in a small saucepan with the flour over a low heat. It should become like a thick, smooth paste. Slowly add the milk and keep stirring until the béchamel becomes thick, like custard. Add salt to taste then set aside.

Finely slice or chop the mushrooms and cook them in a pan with the rest of the butter for 3–5 minutes, or until they are cooked through and soft. At the last minute, squeeze over some lemon juice and sprinkle over the parsley.

Combine the scallops, béchamel and mushrooms – taste and, if needed, adjust for seasoning – and spoon this mixture back into the scallop shells. Sprinkle about ½ teaspoon of breadcrumbs over each and bake them for 10–15 minutes, or until they are bubbling and the tops are golden.

Piatti piccoli

Mushrooms and polenta

Funghi e polenta

IN VENICE FUNGHI E POLENTA IS often made with fresh, meaty porcini mushrooms or *chiodini* (honey fungus) and served on a bed of creamy yellow polenta or, a more old-fashioned way to serve them, as a flan using a small dish such as a ramekin to form *'sformati'* with the mushrooms served around them. Leftovers are perfect on grilled polenta crostini (or regular bread crostini), too. This preparation is lovely with any wild mushroom.

Serves 6

300 g (10½ oz/3⅓ cups) mushrooms
2–3 tablespoons olive oil
2 garlic cloves, finely chopped
a few parsley sprigs, finely chopped
creamy polenta (see page 50), to serve

Trim the mushrooms of any dry or woody stems then dunk in a bowl of fresh water quickly to remove any dirt or debris. If using larger mushrooms, cut them into smaller chunks, otherwise small mushrooms such as chiodini can be left whole.

Heat the olive oil in a wide pan over a low heat and gently fry the garlic until soft and fragrant (be careful not to let it brown), then throw in the mushrooms, still wet, along with a splash of water, some salt and pepper and turn the heat up to medium. Continue cooking until the mushrooms are soft and cooked through. If they are small this will take about 5 minutes. Add the parsley during the last minute, check for seasoning and toss.

Serve with creamy polenta.

Cuttlefish stewed in its ink

Seppie al nero

PILES OF WHITE-FLESHED cuttlefish stained with black ink are a common sight at the Rialto market, where both cuttlefish and its ink sac are valued ingredients and often cooked together. The glossy black ink lends a deliciously briny, even earthy flavour to this dish, but above all, it lends it that deep, dark colour that makes it such a striking dish, especially when served over a bed of pearly white polenta, or stirred through pasta (*bigoli*, thick noodles – the only traditional Venetian noodle – would be ideal) or risotto. While squid ink (which you can also find sold as a separate ingredient, usually in a jar) may seem like an expensive or superfluous ingredient to some now, this is a dish that characterises *cucina povera*, the peasant side of Venice's cuisine – this was once a dish linked to tougher times, when the only thing available to flavour some rice or polenta was the cheap leftover ink after all the squid was already eaten. If you can, choose smaller cuttlefish for this.

Gently heat the olive oil in a wide saucepan and infuse it with the garlic clove for a few minutes, being careful to keep the heat on low so the garlic doesn't burn but only turns slightly golden. Remove the clove, then add the onion and cook until soft and translucent, about 7 minutes or so. Add the cuttlefish and turn the heat up to medium and cook for about 2 minutes, then add the ink, the wine, tomatoes and a good pinch of sea salt and freshly ground pepper. Bring to a simmer, then turn the heat down to low and cover the pan. Let it cook for about 30 minutes, occasionally stirring and checking for tenderness (a fork should easily pierce the cuttlefish like butter). If it begins to look like the sauce has reduced too much, add some water to top it up. At the last minute, stir through the parsley and taste for seasoning, adding more salt or pepper if needed. The onions and cuttlefish make this quite a sweet-tasting dish. Serve over soft white polenta or atop bread or polenta crostini.

Serves 4

60 ml (2 fl oz/¼ cup) olive oil
1 garlic clove, peeled and squashed
1 onion, sliced
300 g (10½ oz) cuttlefish, cleaned
    (see Note) and cut into thin strips
1–2 teaspoons squid ink, or the contents
    of the cuttlefish's own ink sac
125 ml (4 fl oz/½ cup) dry white wine
200 g (7 oz) puréed or peeled tinned
    tomatoes (about half a tin)
a few parsley sprigs, finely chopped
soft white polenta (see page 50) or
    crostini, to serve

NOTE If you have procured some beautiful whole cuttlefish and are planning to use the ink sacs inside, proceed carefully so as not to break them. First, pierce the membrane near the large, flat cuttlefish bone (this should be done with a fingernail) and then you can easily pull out the bone. Without this structure in the way, you should now be able to see the innards through the almost transparent membrane – carefully pierce this (again, a fingernail should do it or you can use a small knife, just be careful not to be too enthusiastic with it). Once you open up the cuttlefish this way, the innards will be exposed and you can find the ink sac right at the bottom, an almost glowing, silvery-blue orb. Gently cut it out and set aside on a plate. Cut and remove the rest of the innards. Cut off the tentacles, avoiding the eyes and beak, which you can discard – you can cut the tentacles in half or leave intact if small. Peel the skin off the cuttlefish, which is most easily done from the wings, which you can pull off too. You should be left with a flap of white cuttlefish flesh that you can now cut into thin strips. If you do not have whole cuttlefish with the ink sac or cannot get cuttlefish ink separately, you can also do this without the ink; you'll simply have a red sauce instead of the characteristic black sauce, but it will still be delicious.

Fresh tuna stewed with tomatoes

Ton fresco in tecia

THIS IS INSPIRED BY a recipe that leapt out at me from a wonderful Venetian cookbook because the recipe begins with 'Buy a good tuna steak at the Rialto...' It is called *A Tola Co I Nostri Veci*, 'At the table with our elders', originally written in 1971 by Mariù Salvatori de Zuliani and in its seventeenth edition. This labour of love was written entirely in the author's native Venetian dialect and is a precious source of historical and more recent recipes and anecdotes. I don't speak Venetian, but I have certainly learned now to understand many of its culinary terms after being utterly absorbed and transported by this fascinating cookbook, which I often read with a glass of wine in hand, to make it feel even more Venetian.

NOTE The tuna should be at least 'two fingers thick'. I find that two thick tuna steaks cut into four large pieces serves four people nicely. If, instead, you want to make this a small plate to share, cut the tuna into bite-sized pieces to serve six to eight. For the tomatoes, you can use any equivalent here – if fresh tomatoes aren't ripe and juicy, try this with peeled tinned tomatoes (which is actually what de Zuliani calls for), but it is equally delicious with about twelve plump, fresh cherry tomatoes, halved. If the tomatoes aren't particularly juicy, a splash of water can help.

Serves 4

400 g (14 oz) fresh tuna, cut into
    large pieces
plain (all-purpose) flour, for dusting
2 tablespoons olive oil
2 tablespoons butter
1 white onion, finely sliced
4 anchovy fillets preserved in oil
3 fresh San Marzano tomatoes
    (or equivalent; see Note),
    roughly chopped
125 ml (4 fl oz/½ cup) white wine
handful of parsley leaves, finely chopped
creamy polenta (see page 50), to serve

Dust the tuna in just enough flour to coat both sides lightly.

Heat the olive oil and butter in a wide frying pan over a low heat and, when the butter has melted, add the sliced onion and cook very gently, stirring occasionally, until the onion is soft and translucent, about 7 minutes. Do not let the onion brown.

Add the anchovies, which should just eventually melt into the onions, followed by the tomatoes and wine, then turn the heat up to medium and bring to a simmer. Season with salt and pepper. When the tomatoes have begun to break down a little and create a bit of a sauce, add the tuna pieces and continue cooking until the fish is just cooked, 5–7 minutes. Scatter with the parsley and serve with some creamy polenta.

Piatti piccoli

Salt cod stewed in tomatoes

Baccalà al pomodoro

THERE ARE SO MANY ways to prepare *baccalà* in a tomato sauce – a dish you might find in old-school *bàcari* or bars but also on family tables on Christmas Eve – that when I first started researching recipes I was so overwhelmed with the variations between family recipes and the little, subtle touches that make them different. There are those who flour the pieces of cod before cooking, those who use *pelati* (whole peeled tomatoes), as opposed to *concentrato* (tomato paste/concentrated purée), or *passata* (puréed tomatoes). Some add white wine, or red. Some cook the fish first in milk. Usually there is an onion in there, sliced, but sometimes just a garlic clove. At times, a few flecks of butter. It could be baked slowly for hours but is most often cooked on the stovetop. Grated cheese, salted sardines, finely chopped parsley, cinnamon, cloves, 'giant' borlotti *giganti* (cranberry) beans (I have to admit, these are an especially appealing addition) may all make an appearance, alone or together. But I think the one thing that unites every single recipe is that the dish must be served with polenta.

Below is a simple version – feel free to adapt with one of the suggestions above – but one thing that makes it special is the cinnamon, so don't be afraid to try just a pinch. It somehow doesn't change the flavour so much as enhances everything about this dish with a subtle, enticing scent.

Serves 4

2 fillets baccalà, pre-soaked (about 500 g/1 lb 2 oz)
1 white onion, finely sliced
2 tablespoons olive oil
125 ml (4 fl oz/½ cup) white wine, or unsalted vegetable stock, or water
1 × 400 g (14 oz) tin peeled or crushed tomatoes
pinch of ground cinnamon
creamy polenta (see page 50), to serve

Remove the skin of the baccalà fillets. This is easiest to do by pulling from the widest part, not the tail, and remove any large bones (there are usually a few, so use your fingers to feel where they may be and pull them out with sturdy tweezers). Cut into bite-sized chunks.

Heat a saucepan over a gentle heat with the onion and olive oil and a pinch of salt. Cook very gently, so that the onion softens and goes a bit transparent, but make sure that it does not colour, about 7 minutes. Pour over the wine and turn the heat up to medium so that it begins to simmer vigorously. After a few minutes, add the tomatoes along with the cinnamon and another pinch of salt and, when it comes back to a simmer, add in the baccalà and turn down the heat a notch, then cook, uncovered, for a further 15–20 minutes, stirring occasionally. Taste for seasoning and adjust with some salt and freshly ground black pepper or white pepper as needed.

Serve with creamy polenta.

Cipriani's carpaccio

Carpaccio alla Cipriani

SOMETIME IN JUNE 1950, this dish was invented by Giuseppe Cipriani of Harry's Bar for his friend and favourite client, the well-known Venetian countess Amalia Nani Mocenigo, who (as the story goes) had been put on a strict diet by her doctor. It included having to avoid cooked meat (there are many different stories as to why this may have been, low red blood cells being one of them, but her granddaughter Barbara Garavelli Nani Mocenigo recounts on her blog that her mother always explained nonna had been poisoned by an anchovy and could never eat cooked meat again). So, the countess couldn't order her usual _entrecôte_, but Giuseppe instead prepared a lean dish of raw prime beef, in the thinnest slices, with a light mayonnaise spiked with mustard and worcestershire sauce. It has been a classic ever since. It was named after the Renaissance Venetian painter (as Cipriani is fond of doing) Vittore Carpaccio, who studied under Bellini (see page 193).

Serves 2 as a light lunch or 3–4 as antipasto

200 g (7 oz) beef fillet
2 egg yolks
1 tablespoon lemon juice
200 ml (7 fl oz) extra-virgin olive oil
½ teaspoon dijon mustard
white pepper, to taste
½ teaspoon worcestershire sauce
1 tablespoon full-cream (whole) milk,
    or as needed

To prepare the beef, make sure it is cleaned of any connective tissue and fat (trim it away if not) so you are left with just the lean meat. Put the fillet in the freezer for 30 minutes so that it is nice and firm.

In the meantime, you can prepare the sauce. Blend the yolks with a pinch of salt and the lemon juice with a hand blender and slowly add the olive oil in a thin stream until it is incredibly creamy and very thick – you may not need it all. Stir through (and adjust to your taste), the mustard, some white pepper, worcestershire sauce and some milk to loosen the sauce to your liking. You may even like to add more lemon juice or more salt. Set aside.

Remove the fillet from the freezer and slice into 3 mm (⅛ in) slices with a very sharp knife, then flatten the slices using the flat side of the knife's blade, using a bit of pressure until you flatten them to about 1–2 mm (¹⁄₁₆ in) thin. This will result in neater, more compact slices than if you batter them with a meat mallet.

Scatter salt over the top (place the salted meat in the fridge to keep well chilled until needed if not serving right away), then serve the Carpaccio with the sauce drizzled over the top. You can also put the sauce in a squeeze bottle so you can decorate the dish 'Kandinsky style' as they like to do in Harry's Bar, in a sort of criss-cross pattern.

NOTE You could easily make this into more of a *cicchetto* by placing small slices of beef onto toasted bread crostini with a drizzle of the sauce over the top. This makes plenty of sauce, you won't need it all, and if using a hand blender or similar you will find it hard to make this mayonnaise in a smaller quantity – but the bright side is that it is absolutely delicious and you will want to eat it with everything you can. It's perfect with fish, with vegetables, and on sandwiches too. It goes without saying that you should use the best-quality beef you can afford.

Piatti piccoli

Venetian-style liver

Fegato alla veneziana

THIS IS A CLASSIC of Venice's cuisine, and much loved throughout Italy. I was immediately drawn to the two recipes that Mariù Salvadori de Zuliani includes in her Venetian cookbook *A Tola Co I Nostri Veci*. One is a recipe from the year 1800 and she claims it is the most authentic recipe for this classic dish, which doesn't use either vinegar or wine, but lemon juice. The other recipe is her own family recipe and she adds that you can use wine – red, or even a sweet one like Marsala – to finish the dish. But some will use beef stock, others just white-wine vinegar. It is really about balancing the sweetness of the onions and liver with the acidity of the wine and vinegar and, to this end, I think the lemon wedges (for guests to adjust the acidity to taste themselves) are a must.

NOTE This is best made with very fresh veal liver, but if you can only find frozen liver, defrost it slowly by placing it in the fridge overnight for best results.

Serves 6

2 tablespoons olive oil
2 tablespoons butter
500 g (1 lb 2 oz) white onions, thinly sliced
500 g (1 lb 2 oz) veal liver, sliced into strips (see Note)
80 ml (2½ fl oz/⅓ cup) white wine or white-wine vinegar
a few parsley sprigs, finely chopped
lemon wedges, to serve
creamy polenta (see page 50), to serve

In a wide, shallow pan, heat the oil and butter together and begin cooking the onion over a low heat with a good pinch of salt until it is very soft, almost creamy, about 15 minutes. Add a splash of water to help the cooking without browning the onion. Add the liver, turn up the heat to medium–high and sear all sides briefly, adding salt and freshly ground pepper. Pour over the white wine, add another pinch of salt and continue cooking for 5 minutes. The liver should be cooked until slightly pink inside. Serve scattered with parsley and lemon wedges over a puddle of soft polenta.

Venetian-style potatoes

Patate alla veneziana

THE PAIRING OF ONIONS with these golden, olive oil–soaked potatoes is quite irresistible to me. Some might compare this to a similar French dish for Lyonnaise-style potatoes, but I can't help but think the use of onions this way is so typically Venetian (and, actually, that before becoming Venetian, it was borrowed from the great exposure to Turkish cuisine, as gastronome Giuseppe Maffioli suggests), where everything from *baccalà* to fried sardines to liver starts out this way. You could serve these in small bowls with a toothpick to fish them out as *cicchetti*. This is as delicious piping hot as it is cold the next day.

Serves 4–6

500 g (1 lb 2 oz) potatoes
1 white onion, thinly sliced
2 tablespoons butter
2 tablespoons extra-virgin olive oil,
  or as needed
handful of parsley leaves, finely chopped

Place the whole potatoes in cold water and bring to a simmer, then par-boil for 15 minutes. Drain. When cool enough to handle, peel and chop the potatoes into chunks (the reason for boiling them whole first is so they aren't too watery for the next step).

Cook the onions in the butter and olive oil in a wide frying pan over a medium heat until they begin to turn soft, about 3–5 minutes. Add the potatoes, a good pinch of salt and some freshly ground pepper, and continue cooking, tossing occasionally, to give the potatoes time to get a nice golden colour. They should be cooked through, while getting a little crisp and browned on the edges and the onions should begin to caramelise, about 7–10 more minutes. You could add some olive oil if you think it needs it. Sprinkle with the parsley at the last minute and adjust for seasoning, adding salt or pepper if you like.

Venetian-style whole spider crab
Granceola alla veneziana

THIS LARGE CRAB, also commonly known as *grancevola* or *granseola*, is often the centrepiece of Venetian restaurants, where it will be flaunted on ice in displays at the front to entice customers. It is, as Mariù Salvatori de Zuliani writes, the most well-known specialty of Venetian cuisine. She notes it is best eaten in the months of November until January, as this is when you can find the females also full of eggs. They must always be cooked live, the long, spider-like legs and claws tied to the body so they don't splash, and the meat is simply dressed with olive oil, salt, pepper and lemon juice. In *I Sapori del Veneto* (2010), Mila Contini notes you should get one male crab and one female crab – the first has tastier meat, the latter has it in more abundance – boiled for exactly 7 minutes, then cracked open, shredded and mixed together. In restaurants, it's often served in the opened shell of the crab itself, turned upside-down like a bowl. The shredded meat is placed inside and the dressing goes over the top, then you only need a fork and a glass of Prosecco.

Friar's wild herb frittata

Frittata dei frati

THIS IS A FRITTATA to prepare in the spring when you can forage for wild herbs. Otherwise, use any regular fresh herbs you like; just remember the key here is to use fistfuls of them – not just as a garnish, but treat the herbs like vegetables.

This is a recipe I read about in a book produced by Slow Food, *Ricette di Osterie del Veneto*, but it is actually a centuries-old preparation. A frittata filled with wild herbs including spinach, mint, sage, marjoram and parsley is in one of the oldest Italian cookbooks, the fourteenth-century *Libro per Cuoco*, written by a Venetian cook, as a recipe intended for *Quaresima*, Lent, where eating meat was forbidden for 40 days until Easter. The Slow Food recipe itself is inspired by the sixteenth-century cookbook *Singolar Dottrina* by Domenico Romoli, a sort of gastronomic encyclopedia of Renaissance Venice from 1560, and it includes a handful of breadcrumbs boiled in wine to thicken the frittata, which is perfumed with cinnamon and white pepper, along with basil, lemon verbena, spearmint and *santoreggia* (winter savory).

I use a combination of wild and regular herbs, such as wild fennel, borage, nettle, *nepitella* (calamint, but you could use a combination of mint and oregano in its place), sage and rosemary. In the Veneto, some other traditional herbs you can find are *bruscandoli* (wild hop shoots), wild radicchio, dandelion and poppy leaves, wild asparagus and wild garlic. Romoli's reference to *frati*, or friars, in the name of this dish I imagine is because Venice's vegetable gardens and green spaces were often found inside monastery walls and the use of herbs in cooking and medicinal concoctions was a specialty of these monasteries. The traditional finish on this frittata is a sprinkle of cinnamon and sugar. It's unusual today, but cinnamon and sugar was a condiment that you'd easily find on Venetian tables that was only relatively recently replaced with grated parmesan. It works beautifully on this herby frittata.

Makes 4 cicchetti

40–50 g (1½–1¾ oz, or two big handfuls)
    fresh wild or regular herbs (see
    opposite for suggestions)
4 eggs, beaten
2 tablespoons grated parmesan
a good grating of fresh nutmeg, or a
    pinch of cinnamon
white pepper, to taste
1 tablespoon butter
1 tablespoon olive oil
1 tablespoon white wine, or water

When you get home from foraging herbs,
place them in a large bowl of cool water
for a while to revive them and keep them
fresh, then let them dry on a tea towel
(dish towel). When ready to cook, chop
the herbs all together very finely (breathe
in the incredible scent!).

Beat the eggs with the parmesan in a small
mixing bowl and add the nutmeg, a good
pinch of salt and some white pepper.

Place the butter and oil in a wide,
non-stick frying pan or cast-iron pan
(something that is good for sliding eggs
around in) over a medium heat. Cook
the herbs for about 1 minute, letting

them sizzle and turn dark green and
glossy. Pour over a splash of white wine,
continue cooking for 1 minute then add
the egg mixture. Swirl to cover the whole
pan and cook until it is set on top – the
egg should still be glistening but not very
wobbly. Slide the frittata gently onto a
plate held in one hand, then place the pan
over the top of the plate and, carefully
but decisively, flip everything together so
that you now have the undercooked side
of the frittata on the bottom of the pan.
Continue cooking for 30 seconds or so,
then flip back onto the plate. Serve warm
or at room temperature, cut into slices,
or as a topping for crusty bread.

Fresh scallops from the Rialto market

At a cafe in Campo Santa Margherita

Dolcie
Bevande
Dolcie
Bevande
Dolcie

Dolci e bevande Sweets and drinks	*Spritz*
	Bellini
	Sgroppino
	Cioccolata calda di Marco Marco's thick hot chocolate
	Marmellata di rose Rose petal jam
	Fritole Venetian Carnival fritters
	Crema fritta Deep-fried custard
	Crema di mascarpone Mascarpone cream
	Bussolai S-biscuits from Burano
	Zaleti di Valeria Valeria's polenta and sultana biscuits
	Pevarini Pepper biscuits
	Pinza di pane Bread pudding
	Torta de pomi Venetian apple cake
	Pan del doge di Zaira Zaira's fruit cake

'Venice is like eating
an entire box of
chocolate liqueurs
in one go.'

Right
Panificio Giovanni Volpe
in the old ghetto is
Venice's only remaining
kosher bakery

Sugar, the powder of Cyprus

Sugar was the status symbol of the elite in the Renaissance – and it was accessible to Venetians more than anyone else in Europe thanks to the fact that they were the first to import this precious, sweet substance. The Venetians first encountered sugar during the Crusades at the end of the eleventh century. Although the Arabs had already introduced sugar to Sicily when it was an Arabic state in the ninth century, it didn't catch on anywhere else. It was the lagoon city that commercialised and then diffused it to the rest of the continent.

The *Libro per Cuoco*, the fourteenth-century cookbook by the 'anonymous Venetian' cook, is filled with recipes influenced by the East, 'a richness of sugar and spices that at the time only Venetians could afford', says Giuseppe Maffioli. According to Giampiero Rorato, until the sixteenth century, however, sugar was still considered a spice in Europe – and spices were, for the most part, treated as medicinal. So, the cost of sugar was exorbitant and it wasn't used for food. Sweetness was usually obtained by adding honey or sultanas, or *mosto*, the leftovers of the wine harvest crushed and boiled into a jammy syrup.

The merchants of Venice kept the price of sugar high throughout the Middle Ages, but as the Venetian Republic expanded their cultivation of sugar cane on their colonies in Cyprus and Crete, and perfected the long and complicated process of creating sugar, it became a more accessible, more common ingredient in the kitchen and on the table. But this happens, notes Carla Coco in *Venezia in Cucina*, for the most part, in the 1700s. *La polvere di Cipro*, the powder of Cyrus, she says, was a must at parties, celebrations and weddings. Venice was full of laboratories that created marzipan, confections, candied almonds and caramelised fruit. Sugar was sprinkled generously over *fritole*, fried treats cooked humbly on the street (see page 202). But it's not just for sweets: the 'imprinting from the Levant and the love for sweet-and-sour [*dolzegarbo* in dialect, much like the many *in saor* preparations] is used in dishes that are served throughout the entire meal – not just at the end', Coco notes. In fact, until recently, Venetian dishes were often finished with a condiment of grated cheese, cinnamon and sugar (see also the unusual sweet, deep-fried meatball recipes in the introduction to *Polpette di carne*, page 130).

Around this time, too, so-called 'colonial drinks' such as tea, coffee and hot chocolate began to appear, all served with sugar in small pots, and teacups and teaspoons that weren't there before became part of the table setting. Meanwhile, cafes – think of decadent Caffè Florian, which opened its doors in magnificent Piazza San Marco in 1720 – filled with the ritual of cafe-goers drinking cups of tea, coffee and chocolate at all times of the day. A ritual revolving around that sugar pot.

Spritz

UNDENIABLY, THE SPRITZ has become one of Italy's – if not the world's – favourite cocktails. And yet just a decade ago it was something you may have only enjoyed when travelling to Italy's north-east, where the drink originated as nothing more than a mixer of white wine and sparkling water (today it's called *spritz bianco*, a white spritz; see Variations). In Venice, the spritz is still the favourite aperitivo of choice and when you ask for one, you'll immediately be asked with which bitters would you like it made – Aperol, Campari or Select, usually, but some also offer bitters such as Cynar, the artichoke digestif, which makes a nice change.

Select, intense pinkish-red and dry, with flavours of juniper berries and rhubarb roots, is the choice of proud Venetians, as it is local (an idea born between the young Pilla brothers in the *sestiere* of Castello in 1920) and, whenever I can, I like to order mine with this too as I find the usual Aperol can be cloyingly sweet. Those who prefer a stronger cocktail and the classic bitter flavour will like the version with Campari.

This is the perfect spritz, served in a tumbler with a whole large green olive (not the kind that have already been pitted) served on the end of a skewer so you can easily fish it out of the glass and nibble on it, but some may like a slice of orange instead.

Makes 1 short spritz

ice, as needed
30 ml (1 fl oz) Select
60 ml (2 fl oz/¼ cup) Prosecco
soda water (club soda), to top up
a large green olive on a skewer, or a slice
   of orange as garnish (optional)

Fill a short tumbler with ice to cool the glass while you gather the ingredients. Tip out any melted ice that may have gathered at the bottom of the glass. Pour over the Select, the Prosecco, then top up with soda water. Serve with an olive, or your preferred garnish. Double this amount if you want to put it in a bigger glass such as a wine glass.

VARIATIONS The Hugo is a delicious variation of the original white wine and sparkling water spritz, most often made with the addition of 20 ml (¾ fl oz) elderflower syrup (lemon balm syrup was the original creation, but admittedly more difficult to procure) and therefore less alcoholic than the better known spritz. A squeeze of lemon is nice in this too. Garnish with mint leaves.

The land of Prosecco

ITALY'S FAVOURITE SPARKLING aperitif is produced in the north-east of the country, in the Veneto and Friuli Venezia Giulia, but the best Prosecco comes from the hills of the Conegliano Valdobbiadene (pronounced 'ko-ne-lee-ah-no val-doh-bee-ah-den-aye') areas in the province of Treviso, a UNESCO World Heritage Site, and this wine is protected with prestigious DOCG (Controlled and Guaranteed Designation of Origin) status, which you will always find as a paper sticker attached to the neck of the bottle. It is worth seeking out as, in comparison, Prosecco labelled DOC is a more basic, mass-produced Prosecco.

Prosecco is actually also the name of the grape variety used in this eponymous wine, but in 2009 was renamed *Glera* (confusing, but this was done so that 'Prosecco' could be registered as a region instead), but it isn't the only grape you will find in the wine – often you can find other rare indigenous varieties such as Verdiso, Bianchetta and Perera making up a small percentage too. What sets Prosecco apart from other sparkling wines is how it is made – yeast and sugar is added to the base wine in very large fermentation tanks. As the wine referments, carbon dioxide is released and the pressure caused by this carbonates the wine. The wine is then filtered and gets a hit of sugar before bottling. Prosecco labelled

Brut is the driest, with the least amount of sugar added, up to 12 g (¼ oz) per litre. Extra Brut has between 12–17 g (¼–½ oz) and then there is Dry, 17–32 g (½–1 oz).

There is also a recent revival of a traditional process known as Prosecco *col fondo* (*fondo* is the sediment that you can find at the bottom of a wine bottle) where the wine is refermented in the bottle. I'm a fan of this style of Prosecco, which is often cloudy but not always. Look for Prosecco labelled Conegliano Valdobbiadene Superiore DOCG.

Unfortunately Prosecco's worldwide popularity (two thirds of it is exported overseas) might also be its environmental downfall. In recent years, prominent figures such as Carlo Petrini, founder of the International Slow Food movement, and the bishop Corrado Pizziolo have spoken out against the alarming rate at which the Prosecco production area is expanding, which is creating a vast monoculture with a great dependency on pesticides. Where possible, look for EU-certified organic Prosecco (represented by a little rectangle with a green leaf in it) and try to find low-intervention producers, such as Bele Casel, Costadilà and Casa Coste Piane.

Prosecco is so loved because it is food-friendly, it's perfect for serving with *cicchetti* or antipasto, and it has very fresh, simple and crisp aromatics. I think as an aperitif it is rather perfect also because it isn't too alcoholic (usually hovering around 10.5–11.5 per cent alcohol). Naturally, you will find this local bubbly all over Venice, often served on its own, but also mixed in drinks, from Spritz to Bellini, as well as in an after-meal form as Sgroppino. Serve it as chilled as possible, in an equally chilled glass.

Dolci e bevande

Bellini

MADE WITH RIPE, BLUSHING white peaches, this light and refreshing cocktail is the perfect summertime aperitivo. The original Bellini was created in the 1930s in Venice's legendary Harry's Bar. It's a simple, elegant drink of local Prosecco (see page 190), stirred gently (so as not to lose fizz) with puréed white Veronese peaches. Giuseppe Cipriani, Harry's founder, named it after the rosy colours famous in the paintings of Venetian Renaissance artist Giovanni Bellini, and it is still one of the most popular things to order at Harry's Bar. The classic ratio is one-part peach purée to three-parts Prosecco. If you are using Saturn (also known as donut) peaches, those beautiful flattened white peaches, then you can use two of them for this recipe.

This is how it is made by my husband, Marco, who before becoming a sommelier was an excellent bartender at the Atrium Bar at the Four Seasons in Florence. He has the following three tips to share:

Everything should be well chilled, from the peach to the Prosecco, to the glass (put the glasses in the freezer for 10 minutes before serving).

Exposure to air can oxidate the fruit, making the peach purée turn brown – avoid this by not preparing the purée too far in advance (in other words, do it on the spot).

Finally, don't be tempted to add anything else.

Serves 2

1 chilled white peach
250 ml (8½ fl oz/1 cup) Prosecco
2 teaspoons caster (superfine) sugar, if needed

Peel and pit the peach. Place the fruit in a blender with half of the Prosecco and, if the peach is a little tart, the sugar, and blend until smooth. Pour into chilled glasses, add the rest of the Prosecco, give it a gentle stir with a spoon and serve immediately.

VARIATIONS If you cannot get white peaches, there are a number of classic variations on the Bellini, where another fresh, seasonal fruit is substituted for the peaches. For example, a Rossini is made with strawberry purée, Puccini with freshly squeezed mandarin juice and Tintoretto with fresh pomegranate seeds and juice. Just don't substitute yellow peaches; it wouldn't look anything like the pink Venetian skies of a real Bellini.

Sgroppino

THIS FROTHY AFTER-DINNER digestif is an age-old refresher that once graced aristocratic Venetian tables, served between courses as a palate-cleanser, particularly when moving between a seafood and a meat dish. Today, you will often see it as an after-dinner drink in place of dessert and it might even be boosted with a splash of vodka. Its name comes from the Venetian word to 'un-knot' or 'to loosen' – in fact, it is a welcome drink to enjoy after a big meal.

Sadly, in many restaurants you may come across it as an industrially produced, pre-mixed slushie-type concoction. It goes without saying the home-made version is far superior. I also like it in an unmixed version, a little like an elegant, adult ice-cream soda, where the Prosecco is topped with a scoop of lemon sorbet (and perhaps reinforced with a shot of vodka). The key to making this is creating a light and smooth-as-silk consistency. A blender makes this very easy, but purists argue that it should be hand-whisked, as the blender melts the sorbet too quickly. I'm all for doing this by hand – it doesn't take long and whisking is no more laborious than cleaning a blender.

If you have access to really good lemon sorbet from an artisan gelateria by all means use that; if not, below you can find a home-made version.

Serves 4–6

HOME-MADE LEMON SORBET
zest from 5–7 medium-sized lemons
300 g (10½ oz) sugar
250 ml (8½ fl oz/1 cup) lemon juice, strained

TO ASSEMBLE
500 ml (17 fl oz/2 cups) Home-made or other good-quality lemon sorbet (see above)
500 ml (17 fl oz/2 cups) Prosecco

For the sorbet, zest the lemons by either peeling them carefully in strips with a vegetable peeler (be careful not to take the white pith, which is bitter) or by grating the lemons with a microplane and place the zest in a saucepan along with the sugar and 300 ml (10 fl oz) water. Bring to the boil to make a simple syrup, stirring until the sugar dissolves. Take off the heat and let it cool, then add the lemon juice.

If you have cut the zest into large strips, remove these (you can let them dry on a baking rack and you have some strips of candied lemon to use in cakes or biscuits or as a garnish); microplaned zest can remain. If you have an ice-cream machine, churn through the machine until the sorbet is creamy and set. If not, pour the cooled mixture into a large, shallow container so that it is not more than about 7.5 cm (3 in) deep. Freeze for

2 hours, then take out the container and give the whole mixture a good stir with a fork or a whisk. Place back in the freezer and, after another 2 hours, stir again. Place back in the freezer for a further hour or two, until it is creamy rather than icy, and can be scooped easily. Give it another stir and it is ready to use.

If you are using store-bought lemon sorbet, remove the sorbet from the freezer about 10 minutes before assembling the cocktail to let it soften slightly. Place the sorbet in a bowl and whisk by hand until creamy, almost like the texture of whipped butter.

Divide the sorbet between glasses – flutes or Martini glasses are perfect for this. Top up with Prosecco, a little at a time, and stir gently until well incorporated and frothy. Serve with a spoon if quite thick.

Dolci e bevande

Marco's thick hot chocolate

Cioccolata calda di Marco

WHEN HE WORKED as a bartender in Florence's best bars long ago, my husband, Marco, perfected this smooth, dark, thick hot chocolate – it's hard to go back to drinking regular hot chocolate after tasting this. In many Italian bars hot chocolate is often made with less cocoa and with the addition of starch (usually cornflour/cornstarch or arrowroot/tapioca flour) to thicken it, but Marco instead likes to use extra cocoa in place of the starch, which naturally equates to a deeper, darker chocolate flavour.

This is quite rich, so you only need a small amount – this recipe makes enough for two teacup-sized hot chocolates, which I think is the perfect size. This is on the not-too-sweet side, so feel free to adjust to your taste, but I do think the whipped cream is essential, especially if you want to feel as if you're sitting in historic, decadent Caffè Florian in Piazza San Marco with one of their iconic hot chocolates *con panna*.

Makes 1 large drink, or 2 smaller drinks

125 ml (4 fl oz/½ cup) pouring (single/
  light) cream
1 tablespoon icing (confectioners') sugar,
  sifted
35 g (1¼ oz) unsweetened cocoa powder,
  sifted
2 tablespoons sugar, or to taste
250 ml (8½ fl oz/1 cup) full-cream
  (whole) milk

Whip the cream with the icing sugar until thick, soft peaks form. Keep chilled in the fridge while you make the hot chocolate.

Combine the cocoa powder and sugar in a small saucepan and add the milk, a little at first, and mix with a spatula or a whisk until you have a thick paste with no more dry bits, then add the rest of the milk, stirring in as you go, until it is smooth. Bring the mixture to a gentle simmer over a low heat and let it cook for about 1 minute while you stir, until it is thickened slightly. Pour into cups, top with some whipped cream – you may not need all of it, but you never know.

Dolci e bevande

Rose petals for breakfast on an Armenian island monastery

I STUDIED FINE ART at university, something that brought me to Florence in my twenties, where I was awarded a scholarship from the Italian embassy to study art restoration. For several weeks over two autumns while doing that second degree, I got the opportunity to work in the Armenian monastery of the island of San Lazzaro in Venice, where in return for food and lodging, I repaired flooded etchings from the monastery's incredible museum collection.

San Lazzaro degli Armeni was a leper colony in the Middle Ages – and this is how the island got its name, after Saint Lazarus, the patron saint of lepers – but by 1601 it lay mostly abandoned other than as a vegetable plot for the cathedral of San Pietro, until 1717 when La Serenissima gave the island to the founder of the Armenian Catholic Mekhitarists to build a monastery. It has since become one of the world's most important centres of Armenian culture. When Lord Byron visited the monastery in 1816 there were seventy

monks at San Lazzaro. When I was there in 2007 and 2008, there were just five. It sits a 15-minute ferry ride from Piazza San Marco, just west of the Lido and neighbouring the island of San Servolo, where you can now find the Venice International University but was previously an island for escaped nuns and the insane.

The island is small and flat – it probably takes a handful of minutes to walk all the way around it – but big enough for the Armenian monastery that sits quietly and proudly on the lagoon, where it houses a church and a stunning cloister, an extensive museum, a publishing house (now in disuse), accommodations, flower and vegetable gardens, olive trees, rose bushes and occasionally an exhibition for the Venice Biennale. Water softly laps around the edges of the monastery and that is about all you can hear except for the occasional speed boat on its way to the Lido.

In the evenings after closing the makeshift laboratory, I would catch the *vaporetto* coming from the Lido, glide into a foggy Piazza San Marco and wander the quiet canals of Venice to my favourite *bàcari*, bridges and squares before heading back to the monastery, like Cinderella, by midnight. But one of my favourite parts of the day was breakfast, when the monks supplied coffee, *fette biscottate* (dried slices of bread), butter and a large, deep-pink jar of their famous rose petal jam, known as *vartanush* – ruby, almost transparent petals floating in a luscious, silky syrup. It is made every May with small, blooming magenta flowers, picked at sunrise. The monastery is open for guided visits once a day for visitors coming in on the *vaporetto* from Piazza San Marco, and this is the chance to get a jar of their special rose petal jam – but it is produced in limited quantities and they disappear quickly off the gift-shop shelves.

Rose petal jam

Marmellata di rose

WHILE THE ARMENIAN monks of San Lazzaro did not reveal their exact recipe to me, one thing that they did share was their special technique: the petals have to be massaged to soften them and get the most out of that beautiful rose perfume and fuchsia colour. I've long used a recipe from Pellegrino Artusi's 1891 cookbook as inspiration; he loves using *'rosa dalla borraccina'* (also known as *rosa centifolia*, literally 'hundred-leaved' rose, or cabbage rose, as they are known above all for their sweet fragrance and rose oil), but I'm quite convinced the success of making a rose petal jam as special as the one from San Lazzaro island depends on the roses themselves, which should be small, deep pinkish-red roses with thin petals, perfumed and freshly picked, not at all wilted or old. It is also important to choose rose petals that you know have not been sprayed, for example from someone's garden. Do not use commercial roses for this. For this recipe you will need about two large mixing bowls full of petals.

Makes 750 ml (25½ fl oz/approx. 3 cups) jam

200 g (7 oz) freshly picked rose petals
juice of 1 lemon
600 g (1 lb 5 oz/2¾ cups) sugar

Gently rinse the rose petals and lay them on a tea towel (dish towel). Use another tea towel to carefully dab them to remove some of the excess moisture. Place them in a large mixing bowl with the lemon juice and about 200 g (7 oz; approximately 1 cup) of the sugar. Rub and carefully 'massage' the petals with the sugar and juice until they are no longer velvety but limp (still whole, however) and the mixture begins to look like a pulp. Set aside.

Place the rest of the sugar in a saucepan with 625 ml (21 fl oz/2½ cups) water. Bring to a simmer over a medium heat and cook until the sugar is dissolved. Add the massaged rose petals and continue simmering until the syrup thickens slightly and the petals no longer float, stirring occasionally. This takes about 30 minutes.

Note that this jam is not the same consistency as a traditional jam, but rather it is a perfumed syrup with softened, delicate petals in it. A saucer test will help you quickly see if the jam is ready: place a saucer in the freezer before you start and when you want to test the jam, add a small blob of it to the cold saucer. As it cools down, quickly look at how the syrup behaves when you turn the plate to let it run (it should run slower than water, as it will be slightly thickened). Be careful not to overcook the syrup as it will harden.

Transfer the hot jam to sterilised glass jars, fill to the top, seal tightly and leave to cool. If instead you are filling the jars with cooled jam, once sealed, place them in a saucepan filled with water right up to the neck of the jar and boil for 5 minutes to help seal the jar completely, then let cool. Store in a cool, dry place until opened and then store in the fridge, where it should be consumed within a few weeks. I particularly love this rose petal jam drizzled over thick yoghurt or ricotta.

Venetian Carnival fritters

Fritole

DECLARED THE OFFICIAL dessert of Venice in the eighteenth century, sugar-crusted *fritole* (which are similar to doughnut holes but are studded with dried and candied fruit and nuts, and rolled in sugar) were also called the 'Queen of Venetian pastry-making' by early twentieth century Venetian journalist Elio Zorzi. It's interesting when you delve into this beloved treat – which was sold piping hot in the streets, *'Calde calde calde le ga a boaa'*, as the call of *fritoleri* announced – that they are also the perfect example of how Venetian cuisine was so uniquely marked by the lagoon city's important relationship with the *Levante*, which in medieval Venice referred, in particular, to Syria-Palestine, Egypt, Turkey and even Greece.

In Giampiero Rorato's *Origini e Storia della Cucina Veneziana* (2010), the journalist points to a work by an eleventh-century physician from Baghdad known in Europe as Ibn Jazla. His tome was translated into Latin in 1280 by the Jewish-Sicilian doctor Faraj ben Salem and there are a number of Persian recipes, including one for *Zelabia*, also described by Giambonino da Cremona in *Liber de ferculis et condimentis* ('the book of dishes and condiments', which is essentially a collection of Jazla's Arabic recipes, translated by Giambonino in the thirteenth century) as a yeasted batter where small portions are fried by the spoonful in oil or lard and covered in honey. A century later, in the *Libro per Cuoco* written by the 'anonymous Venetian cook', recipe twenty-eight is for *frittelle bianche*, 'white fritters' that are made with a yeasted batter that includes almond flour (ground almonds) and are covered in sugar. This is an important – and specifically Venetian – case, to see sugar at this time rather than honey (see Sugar, the powder of Cyprus, page 187).

Fast forward to the sixteenth century and we find *'Zelabia'* again in an account by Andrea Alpago, a Venetian physician to the consulate in Syria reporting on foods, medicines and other products, described as a spongy, soft pastry fried in oil and eaten with sugar or honey and found throughout Egypt and Syria. And in Bartolomeo Scappi's *Opera* (1570) there is a recipe for *frittelle alla veneziana*, Venetian-style fritters, where goat's milk, butter, rosewater and saffron are mixed with flour into a dough before eggs are added and the batter is fried in lard, then served hot, covered in sugar.

Around the time of Gaetano Zompini's etching of a Venetian street-side *fritole*-maker, *Le Arti che Vanno per Via*, was printed, Pietro Longhi painted a similar scene, *La Venditrice di Fritole* (1755), which is displayed in Ca' Rezzonico, one of the most beautiful palaces (and home of the Museum of eighteenth century Venice) on the Grand Canal. In this outdoor scene, a woman is stooped over a pot of fritters, stringing the *fritole* onto a long skewer; her young helper is holding a large bowl of fritters to the side, while the customers seem to be ordering three skewers, indicated by a simple hand gesture.

Shortly after Zompini's etchings were printed, Carlo Goldoni (see page 53) released a new theatrical comedy, *Il Campiello* (one of Goldoni's most celebrated works), set and written in celebration of Venice's Carnival, featuring a proud Venetian seller of *fritole*, Orsola. One can only imagine that the character of Orsola, like the women in Longhi's and Zompini's artworks, in her dress with its large apron, crouched over a bubbling pot of fritters, depicted faithfully a truly beloved part of Venice's everyday life.

Although the peddlers selling their freshly fried *fritole* on street corners in Venice are no longer, every single bakery and pastry shop in the city makes sure no one goes through Carnival season without the offer of *fritole* still on street corners or *campi*. Traditionally made in copious amounts to feed an army (judging by the list of ingredients in old recipes) with a yeasted batter of eggs, flour, milk, grappa or rum, and usually dotted with sultanas, candied citron and pine nuts, these days you'll find many more kinds on offer, filled with ricotta, *crema* (custard), rice, thinly sliced apples or even zabaione.

Some don't add sugar to the dough at all, only coating it generously after they are fried. Very traditional recipes might leave out the eggs. Lemon zest is common too, especially if you decide to leave out the candied citron (and adds so much fragrance to the warm fritters). Many of the traditional recipes (before the time of electric mixers) call for working the dough tirelessly for 30–45 minutes with a wooden stick – but this loose batter produces puffy, fluffy *fritole* with the ease of a simple hand whisk.

Makes approx. 16

80 g (2¾ oz/½ cup) sultanas
60 ml (2 fl oz/¼ cup) grappa, or rum
15 g (½ oz) fresh yeast (or 3.5 g/0.12 oz
    active-dried yeast)
125 ml (4 fl oz/½ cup) lukewarm
    full-cream (whole) milk
1½ tablespoons butter, melted and cooled
2 eggs, at room temperature
1 tablespoon sugar, plus extra for rolling
    them in
zest of 1 lemon
½ teaspoon salt
200 g (7 oz/1⅓ cups) plain (all-purpose)
    flour
30 g (1 oz) pine nuts (optional)
vegetable oil, for frying (see page 118
    for tips)

Place the sultanas in the grappa and let them soak until needed (alternatively, you can soak them in warm water if you prefer).

Crumble the fresh yeast (or mix the dried yeast) into the lukewarm milk and mix until creamy. Tip this into a large bowl and whisk in the melted butter and the eggs until combined, then add the sugar, lemon zest and salt. Whisk in the flour just until you have a sticky but smooth batter rather like thick pancake batter.

Cover the dough and let it rise in a warm place (such as inside the oven with the pilot light on, or next to a heater if you are doing this in the dead of winter, as is traditional for Carnival) for about 2 hours, or until doubled in size. Add the sultanas and their grappa (or drain them if not using the grappa) and stir them into the batter along with the pine nuts, if using.

Heat enough oil in a saucepan over a medium heat so it is at least 5–7 cm (2–2¾ in) deep.

Prepare a cooling rack with a few sheets of absorbent kitchen paper and place the extra sugar in a bowl.

When the oil reaches about 160°C (320°F) – if you don't have a candy thermometer you can also look for the visual cues described on page 118 – using two spoons to help you, pick up blobs of batter and carefully drop the batter into the hot oil. Fry a few at a time, being careful not to overcrowd the pan. Let them cook, turning them on all sides until evenly deep golden brown; you want to make sure the dough is cooked all the way through, which takes 3–4 minutes. When ready, first drain them on the absorbent kitchen paper for a moment, then, while still piping hot, roll them in the sugar (alternatively, you can dust them in icing/ confectioners' sugar later). These are divine while still warm, but you can also serve them at room temperature. They are best on the day they are made.

Dolci e bevande

Deep-fried custard

Crema fritta

FRIED CUSTARD IS A specialty of the Venetian *Carnevale* (Carnival), and from the 17th January for the feast day of Anthony the Great until *Martedì grasso* (Mardi Gras) you can find these sugar-crusted golden cubes in Venice's bakeries, pastry shops and *bàcari*. Sometimes they are even made with sweet polenta cooked in milk until creamy instead of custard. Loved by adults and children alike for good reason, grown-ups might like these particularly with a glass of dessert wine.

Makes 16

2 whole eggs
2 egg yolks
200 g (7 oz) sugar
120 g (4½ oz) plain (all-purpose) flour
500 ml (17 fl oz/2 cups) full-cream
     (whole) milk
zest of 1 lemon
1 teaspoon vanilla extract
100 g (3½ oz/1 cup) dry breadcrumbs
vegetable oil, for frying

Separate the eggs and set aside the whites for later. Whisk the four egg yolks directly in a heavy-bottomed saucepan with half (100 g/3½ oz) of the sugar. Add the flour and whisk again to a smooth, thick paste. Add the milk, bit by bit at the beginning, until you have a smooth, fluid mixture. Add the lemon zest and vanilla and, finally, place the saucepan over a low heat. Using a wooden spoon or a whisk, keep an eye on the custard as it heats, stirring slowly but constantly to ensure it doesn't catch at the bottom (the edges of the pan are the first place it will start to thicken). Once the mixture begins to thicken, you will need to stir more frequently to ensure it stays smooth, and keep stirring until it is quite thick and semi-solid – the custard should hold its shape. This should take about 20 minutes.

Scrape the custard out of the saucepan and into a buttered, rectangular shallow dish (something like a brownie pan is ideal) and let this mixture cool completely, covered. You can do this the day before and leave it overnight in the fridge if you prefer. Once cooled, cut the custard into 16 squares, around 3 × 3 cm (1¼ × 1¼ in), or whatever makes the most sense in your pan.

Whisk together the two egg whites set aside from earlier in a shallow bowl. In another shallow bowl, place the breadcrumbs. Dip the cubes of custard first into the egg white to cover all sides and then into the breadcrumbs the same way and place them on a clean plate until all the custard is crumbed.

Prepare another shallow bowl with the rest of the sugar.

Place enough oil in a small saucepan to cover the cubes of custard (about 4 cm/1½ in deep, minimum) and heat over a medium heat. It should be about 160°C (320°F), or, if you don't have a candy thermometer, you can test the oil by dipping the end of a wooden spoon into it – it should bubble like Prosecco immediately. Fry the custard in small batches for about 90 seconds, or until they are golden brown. Drain on kitchen paper briefly then toss the hot fried custard into the sugar, rolling it on all sides to coat. You must do this while the custard is piping hot or the sugar won't stick. You can serve immediately or even enjoy them at room temperature, but these are best eaten on the day they are made.

Mascarpone cream

Crema di mascarpone

BEFORE TIRAMISU OR 'tiramesù' was invented in 1970 at the restaurant Alle Beccharie in nearby Treviso, there was always _crema di mascarpone_, the simplest preparation of sweet, creamy mascarpone that has a few similarities with zabaione, another creamy northern Italian favourite for the dipping of biscuits. This is the recipe I have been using since I first tasted a family friend's tiramisu as a teenager (in fact, if you triple this you'll have enough for a three-layer tiramisu made with savoiardi dipped in coffee). Many traditional recipes, such as those of Giuseppe Maffioli in _La Cucina Trevigiana_ (1983) and Mariù Salvatori de Zuliani in _A Tola Co I Nostri Veci_, call for just the egg yolk, which makes a slightly richer, less pillowy _crema_. De Zuliani suggests a splash of rum, if you like, and serving it in Murano glass-stemmed bowls – naturally.

Serve it with fresh strawberries in the spring and summer, over pandoro at Christmas time, or on its own, eaten with a spoon, or for dunking biscuits anytime. Baicoli are particularly Venetian biscuits, ones that no one makes anymore because the Colussi company make such perfect Baicoli that still come in attractive, vintage-looking tins, and they are rather perfect for dipping in sweet mascarpone – small, thin and crunchy, and not too sweet.

Serves 3–4

1 very fresh egg, at room temperature
2 tablespoons sugar, or to taste
150 g (5½ oz) mascarpone
biscuits for dipping, such as Baicoli,
    or fruit such as strawberries

Separate the yolk and the white into two medium bowls. Whip the egg white (make sure you use a very clean bowl – glass or metal is best – and very clean beaters to quickly get beautifully stiff whites) until you have stiff peaks that hold their shape even when you turn the bowl upside-down. Set aside while you whisk the sugar into the egg yolk and add the mascarpone until combined. Fold the whipped egg white into the mascarpone mixture. Chill completely before serving in small bowls with biscuits or fruit to dip.

This is best eaten on the day, or the next at most.

NOTE This recipe uses raw eggs, so it is important that you have very fresh, organic, free-range eggs – if that isn't already your norm. You could pasteurise the eggs if you are squeamish about using them raw, but in Italy the classic way is the simplest way, with fresh eggs. If you can remember to let your egg come to room temperature before using, you will have maximum fluffiness.

Dolci e bevande

Bussolai

THE NAME OF THESE biscuits that are associated with the colourful island of Burano comes from the Venetian word *buso*, or *buca* in Italian, meaning hole. The original *bussolai* were made simply of bread dough (water, flour, yeast and salt) and shaped into the characteristic ring and baked, after which they could easily last three months if kept well in a biscuit tin – no wonder, then, they were the preferred snack of the mariners and fishermen from Burano.

These beloved, long-lasting bread rings were eaten by all Venetians (they are also known as *buranei*, or *buranelli*, referring to their origins on the island of Burano), as they were eventually prepared by the bakeries run by Serenissima apparently as early as the fifteenth century. They took the place of regular fresh bread during meals and were dipped into wine.

But *bussolai* today are usually in the form of sweet biscuits, rich in egg yolks, buttery and sweet (a recipe for *bussolà* in the fourteenth-century *Libro per Cuoco* written by 'a Venetian cook' describes a baked good somewhere between a bread and a biscuit, with eggs, salt, flour and honey). They can still be found in rings, but also in an S-shape, according to some stories, at the request of a restaurateur on Burano, which made them easier to dip into small glasses of sweet wine – these *esse*-shaped ones have since become more popular.

Carol Field has a recipe for *buranelli* in her brilliant book *The Italian Baker*, where her irresistible introduction reads, 'Close your eyes and picture the water stretching away from Venice, past the palazzi and gondolas on the Grand Canal, and think about finding your way to the island of Burano that lies beyond Venice, where these S-shaped buttery cookies are made'. She creams 125 g (4½ oz/½ cup) soft, unsalted butter with almost double the amount of sugar and five egg yolks, perfuming the batter generously with 2 teaspoons vanilla extract and the zest of two lemons, adding flour and salt and shaping into Ss. It is quite similar to the way they are made at Cantina Do Spade, an excellent *bàcaro* near the Rialto market, which is where I have adapted this recipe from.

Makes 16

100 g (3½ oz/⅓ cup plus 1 tablespoon) unsalted butter, softened
100 g (3½ oz/scant ½ cup) sugar
zest of 2 lemons
4 egg yolks
250 g (9 oz/1⅔ cups) plain (all-purpose) flour

Cream the butter and sugar together in a bowl and add the sugar, lemon zest, and then the egg yolks, one at a time. Beat until you have a smooth and creamy mixture. Fold in the flour and mix carefully (I use a spatula here) until the dough comes together. Cover the bowl and place the dough in the fridge to chill for at least 30 minutes or overnight.

Heat the oven to 180°C (350°F). Split the dough into four pieces and roll these into long snakes, about the width of your finger. Break off 15 cm (6 in) lengths and form into an inverted S or a ring shape – or both. Bake until just cooked – about 15 minutes. They should still be pale, just starting to turn golden. Place on a wire baking rack, where they will harden as they cool.

Rizzardini, Venice's oldest pastry shop, opened in 1742

The colourful houses of Burano

Zaleti di Valeria

VALERIA NECCHIO IS A kindred spirit and an old friend. I have always admired her writing, her knowledge and appreciation for food and traditions, and her careful, beautiful photography. Valeria was born and bred in the Venetian countryside, and her cookbook, *Veneto*, is an ode to her homeland. To celebrate it when it was published, we went to Venice to clink many glasses of Prosecco together.

We wandered the *calli* of Venice for hours, to the sound of water lapping at the edges of the canals, and visited the markets, of course, and hopped to and from beloved *bàcari* to eat morsels of *baccalà mantecato*, boiled eggs with anchovies and *sarde in saor*, before visiting a favourite restaurant of hers, Anice Stellato, in a gloriously quiet corner of Cannaregio, where we sat by the canal and had a meal of seared scallops with candied lemon and spaghetti with scampi, washed down with a carafe of unfiltered Prosecco. And when we got home, a plate of her delightful *zaleti* were waiting for us. These plump yet light and crumbly hand-formed polenta biscuits, studded with sultanas, are a love of mine. I could eat them all the time – and Valeria's are the best.

The name *Zaleti*, also known as *zaeti* in dialect, comes from the word *gialetti*, from *giallo*, or yellow, for the presence of yellow polenta, which gives the biscuits a unique, crumbly crunch – use what is known as 'fioretto', or very finely ground polenta. The rest changes from household to household. Valeria says this was the recipe her mum – who was *not* fond of baking – would make when she couldn't be bothered to swing past the bakery. In other words, it is foolproof. Try them with a glass of sweet wine, such as Malvasia or Moscato.

Makes approx. 26

80 g (2¾ oz/½ cup) sultanas
60 ml (2 fl oz/¼ cup) grappa, or water
280 g (10 oz) plain (all-purpose) flour
250 g (9 oz/1½ cups) fine 'fioretto' polenta (cornmeal)
½ teaspoon baking powder
180 g (6½ oz/⅔ cup plus 1 tablespoon) unsalted butter, chilled and diced
2 whole eggs
2 egg yolks
150 g (5½ oz/⅔ cup) caster (superfine) sugar
icing (confectioners') sugar, for dusting (optional)

Soak the sultanas in the grappa for at least 15 minutes, then drain.

In a large bowl, combine the flour, polenta, a pinch of salt and the baking powder and rub this mixture through the butter with your fingers until you have a mixture that resembles damp sand. Beat in the eggs and the yolks, then the sugar, and bring the dough together – you might find this easiest with your hands. Finally, tip in the drained sultanas and combine well. Chill the dough in the fridge for 1 hour.

When ready to bake, heat the oven to 180°C (350°F). Use a heaped tablespoon-sized piece of dough and form it into a thick oval. Place on a baking sheet lined with baking paper and flatten it a little. Leave at least 4 cm (1½ in) space between the biscuits as they will puff up a bit.

Bake for 15–17 minutes – they should be golden and slightly cracked on top but not browned and definitely still a little soft inside. Cool on a wire baking rack and, if you like, dust them with icing sugar before serving. They last well for 2 weeks in an airtight container.

Dolci e bevande

Pepper biscuits

Pevarini

THESE WARM, SPICY, not-too-sweet biscuits are rich in molasses, which substitutes sugar entirely in this recipe and is what also gives them their deep brown colouring and mellow, balsamic-like flavour. They are named for the presence of _pevare_, or pepper, in Venetian dialect – this is white pepper to be precise – and often the recipe is accompanied by other spices too, such as cinnamon, nutmeg and cloves. You could use a combination of them here too. Originally, these would have been made with lard in place of the butter or sometimes brushed with a sticky glaze of simple syrup when coming out of the oven. This is inspired mostly by a recipe from Giampiero Rorato's _I Dolci delle Venezie_ (2005).

Makes approx. 35

350 g (12½ oz/2⅓ cups) plain (all-purpose) flour
1½ teaspoons baking powder
1½ teaspoons ground white pepper
½ teaspoon ground cinnamon
250 g (9 oz/¾ cup) molasses
75 g (2¾ oz/⅓ cup) unsalted butter, softened
juice of ½ lemon
1 egg
cocoa powder, for dusting

Place all the dry ingredients, except for the cocoa powder, in a large bowl. In a separate bowl, beat the molasses, the butter and lemon juice until caramel-like. Add the egg then stir (I like a wooden spoon or a fork) into the flour mixture until you have a well-combined dough.

Rest the dough for 30 minutes in the fridge, or even overnight.

When ready to bake, preheat the oven to 180°C (350°F). Then, on a clean surface such as a wooden board, roll the dough to about 5 mm (¼ in) thick (dust it beforehand with cocoa powder if it is sticky; this will help, like flour, for it to not stick but the colour blends in better). Cut into diamonds approximately 5 cm (2 in) wide and place, spaced well apart, on a baking sheet lined with baking paper.

Bake for 15 minutes, or until the biscuits are slightly puffed and dry on top. Cool on a wire baking tray. They keep well stored in an airtight container for up to 3 weeks. Try these dipped in wine.

Dolci e bevande

Bread pudding

Pinza di pane

THIS IS AN ANCIENT RECIPE – possibly
the most ancient of the Venetian dessert
repertoire – that has a special role for
the Epiphany, on 6th January, and the
start of Venice's Carnival season. As old
traditions went, young singles on this
day had to eat a slice of _pinza_ in seven
different houses to guarantee getting
married within the year.

As it is a homely dish, and one that
makes good use of leftovers or whatever
you have on hand, you can find _pinza_
made with all kinds of grains as the
base – polenta is very common, but also
buckwheat, regular flour or stale bread.

I have a soft spot for bread puddings,
and this is my favourite version, closely
followed by the polenta one. Like the
Pan del doge di Zaira (page 222), you'll
find it studded with dried fruit (usually
figs and sultanas), which sometimes
may have been the only sweet
contribution in this pudding, and nuts
of all kinds, some sort of liquid, be it
milk with a splash of white wine, grappa
or Alkermes, but also an array of spices
such as wild fennel seeds, cinnamon or
nutmeg. It's quite a soft pudding, not
too dense, no matter what it is made
with, perfumed with citrus and fennel,
full of dried figs and sultanas, and it is
to be washed down with a glass of sweet
wine, such as Marsala.

Serves 10

250–300 g (9–10½ oz) stale bread
(about half a large country-style loaf)
500–750 ml (17–25½ fl oz/2–3 cups)
warm full-cream (whole) milk
150 g (5½ oz/1 cup) sultanas
60 ml (2 fl oz/¼ cup) grappa, or rum
or white wine
2 eggs
80 g (2¾ oz/⅓ cup) sugar
60 g (2 oz/¼ cup) butter, melted,
plus extra for greasing
1 teaspoon fennel seeds, bashed slightly
in a mortar and pestle
zest of 1 orange
zest of 1 lemon
150 g (5½ oz/1 cup) dried figs, roughly
chopped
icing (confectioners') sugar, for dusting
(optional)

NOTE The quantity of milk you will need will
depend on the texture of your bread and how
stale it is. Start with 500 ml (17 fl oz/2 cups)
and if it is quite stale, leave it to soak, even
overnight, and you may need to add 250 ml
(8½ fl oz/1 cup) more milk. It should be easy
to crumble or mash.

Tear or cut up the bread (whether you
leave crusts on or off is up to you, but
you should end up with a total of about
250–300 g/9–10½ oz) and let it soak in
500 ml (17 fl oz/2 cups) warm milk until
you can easily crumble or mash the
bread – add more milk if needed, or leave
overnight (see Note).

Preheat the oven to 180°C (350°F).

While the bread is soaking, place the
sultanas in a bowl to steep in the grappa.
If not using alcohol, simply use water.

Stir the bread with its leftover milk
with a wooden spoon (it should break
up easily) – you could also use a food
processor – until you have a dense,
crumbly sort of batter. In a separate
bowl, whisk the eggs and sugar together
with the butter. Add the fennel seeds
and zests and then, with a spoon or
spatula, fold in the bread mixture until
it is creamy and well combined. Add the
sultanas (with their grappa) and the figs
and combine.

Grease a baking tin with butter and line
with baking paper or dust with flour (this is
such a homely recipe, use whatever tin you
have, a springform round cake tin around
22–25 cm/8¾–10 in wide, or a 23 cm/9 in
square tin, like a brownie tin, would work
perfectly. I've even done this in an oval
ceramic dish). Bake for 35–45 minutes, or
until the pudding is golden brown and set.
It should feel firm on top. Serve warm or
cold, dusted with icing sugar before serving,
if you wish. Keep any leftovers in the fridge
for up to 3 days.

Dolci e bevande

Venetian apple cake

Torta de pomi

RATHER THAN A CAKE, this dessert is really just sliced apples held together with the smallest amount of batter. It's reminiscent of a thin French clafoutis and it is absolutely delicious. It is a classic, home-style dessert, for making when you really don't have much around except a lot of apples – in fact, it also goes by the name _torta economica de pomi_ in Mariù Salvatori de Zuliani's book: yes, an economical apple cake. If using particularly sweet apples, I would even cut out a tablespoon of sugar; if using very tart apples, you may like to add an extra one to the batter.

Serves 6–8

1 kg (2 lb 3 oz) apples
3 tablespoons sugar, plus extra for dusting
zest and juice of 1 lemon
2 eggs
2 tablespoons plain (all-purpose) flour, plus extra for dusting
125 ml (4 fl oz/½ cup) full-cream (whole) milk
butter, for greasing

Preheat the oven to 180°C (350°F).

Peel and slice the apples and place them in a bowl with the sugar and lemon juice to marinate while you prepare the rest. In a small bowl, mix the lemon zest, eggs, flour and milk until smooth.

Prepare a ceramic dish or a round cake tin (like the _Pinza di pane_, page 218, this is the homeliest of dishes, so use what you have but don't try this with a springform tin; the batter is quite thin and you'll risk it leaking out! I have tried this in many different-sized and -shaped dishes and I personally prefer my widest ceramic pie dish, which is 26 cm/10¼ in, for a thin layer but you may prefer something smaller for a slightly thicker result). Grease the dish with butter and dust with about a spoonful of flour and sugar each, tapping the dish or tin to distribute evenly. Tip out the excess. Arrange the apple slices and their marinade over the bottom of the dish and pour over the batter. It will seem like very little batter and the apples may stick out from the top, but they will cook down.

Bake for 25–35 minutes (even up to 40 minutes, depending on the apples used), or until the apples are very soft (a toothpick poked through the centre of the cake will help determine this) and golden brown on top. If the apples poking out on top are getting too brown, cover with some aluminium foil until ready. This is rather lovely with a dollop of mascarpone (or thick cream or clotted cream, if you don't have it). Keep any leftovers refrigerated.

Zaira's fruit cake

Pan del doge di Zaira

I ADORE FRUIT CAKES of any kind and the first time I tasted the *pan del doge* from Pasticceria Dal Mas, an historic bakery shop that I somehow found time to nip into as I was running to catch the last train back to Florence, I was hooked.

This cake (pictured on page 224), full of dried and candied fruit and nuts, is found all over Venice, any time of the year. It's so named because the first stories of this 'doge's bread' date back to the doge Silvestro Valier (1630–1700) who supposedly ate it in Villadose, a small town near Rovigo, about 50 km (31 miles) south-west of Venice where he was served this 'bread' (originally it would have been a leavened sweet dough, akin to panettone, but today it is more of a cake), sweetened with honey and full of the ingredients often associated with the Christmas season: candied fruit, dried sultanas and figs, and nuts such as walnuts. In the pastry shops in Venice, you may see this as a log-shaped treat, somewhere between a crumbly cake and a soft biscuit, and other times a round but rather flat cake, sometimes studded on top with blanched almonds, or coated in a generous dusting of powdered icing (confectioners') sugar for appeal.

As soon as I brought this precious package back to Florence and tasted the delicious, fragrant cake, I knew I needed to re-create it and luckily my friend Zaira had a recipe for me – and it was even better than Dal Mas'. Zaira Zarotti is an artist, born into a family of artists in Venice, who seems to have come

from another time. She is Artemisia Gentileschi with a camera. Together with her partner, Francesco, they produce beautiful raku ceramics (you'll spot them in these pages) and the two of them are often found on the Venetian lagoon, in their boat, Zaira's long auburn hair flowing like she's a figure out of a John Everett Millais painting, or dressing up and creating portraits next to dilapidated Palladian-style villas in the countryside. They are the most romantic Venetians I know. Zaira is also a wonderful food writer and storyteller, and this cake of hers – which will delight you as it is baking by perfuming your house with citrus zest, honey and toasting nuts – is my favourite version of this historic treat. I have only tweaked it ever so slightly to reduce the batter a bit so that it is bursting with fruit and nuts, because that is the part for which I am most greedy.

VARIATIONS You can substitute any dried fruit or nuts that you prefer – dried figs, walnuts, hazelnuts, candied citron (which Zaira calls for) or other candied fruit. You could add a splash of rum (why not some of the rum used for soaking the sultanas?) or grappa, if you prefer, or you can leave it out. If you don't have rum to soak the sultanas, substitute with white wine or simply use water. If you would like to put whole almonds on top, as some pastry shops do in Venice, you'll need another 50 g (1¾ oz/⅓ cup) to cover the top of the batter before putting the cake in the oven.

Serve 8–12

100 g (3½ oz) sultanas
125 ml (4 fl oz/½ cup) rum, or water
160 g (5½ oz/⅔ cup) unsalted butter,
 softened, plus extra for greasing
80 g (2¾ oz/⅓ cup) sugar
1½ tablespoons honey
2 eggs
finely grated zest of 1 orange, or lemon
200 g (7 oz/1⅓ cups) plain (all-purpose)
 flour, plus extra for dusting
1 teaspoon baking powder
50 g (1¾ oz/⅓ cup) almonds,
 roughly chopped
40 g (1½ oz/¼ cup) pine nuts
50 g (1¾ oz/¼ cup) candied orange,
 roughly chopped
1 teaspoon vanilla extract
dusting of icing (confectioners') sugar
 (optional)

Preheat the oven to 180°C (350°F). Grease with butter and dust with flour a 23 cm (9 in) baking tin with a springform base.

Place the sultanas in a small bowl with the rum and let them soak for at least 15 minutes.

In a large bowl, whip together the butter, sugar and honey until combined, then add the eggs, one at a time. Add the orange zest and fold through the flour, baking powder and a pinch of salt. Tip in the nuts, candied orange and the soaked sultanas, drained (you could add a splash of the rum too, if you like) and, finally, the vanilla and fold with a spatula until the ingredients are well incorporated.

Tip the batter into the prepared baking tin and smooth out the top. Bake for about 35 minutes, or until the top is deep golden brown and the cake's surface is springy when touched. If you like, dust the top with some icing sugar once cool. There won't be many leftovers once you taste how delicious this cake is, but it does keep well at room temperature for several days, covered.

Dolci e bevande

Pan del doge di Zaira

By the Rialto market

Resources

This is a useful but by no means exhaustive list of international sources for harder-to-find ingredients, from squid ink to fine 'fioretto' polenta (cornmeal) to stockfish.

Stockfish, which is produced exclusively in Norway, is a little bit difficult to buy outside of certain regions in Italy, most notably the Veneto and Calabria, but also Liguria, Sicily and Campania. In Tuscany, it is also used in Livorno, and in Le Marche it is a specialty of Ancona, so there are some other pockets here and there (Italy consumes two-thirds of the Norwegian production of stockfish!). Note that outside of Italy dried stockfish is more commonly found in Italian specialty shops during Christmas or Easter as an important ingredient in popular, traditional festive dishes.

In Australia

Mediterranean Wholesalers

Melbourne's go-to shop for all things Italian. Here you can find stockfish, *baccalà* and liqueurs, plus a deli counter of regional Italian cheeses and cured meats.

mediterraneanwholesalers.com.au

That's Amore Cheese

Local Melbourne producers of Italian-style cheeses. Highly recommended for the *squacquerone* (a soft, delicately tangy cheese), plus aged and specialty cheeses ideal for a *cicchetti* plate.

thatsamorecheese.com.au

IGA Gervasi Thomastown

A neighbourhood Melbourne supermarket where you can find a particularly good selection of Italian ingredients, including *baccalà*.

Preston Market

One of Melbourne's best markets with a selection of fishmongers for *baccalà* and specialty Italian shops, in particular Farinacci deli and Lemnos deli for, among their brimming counters, dried stockfish.

prestonmarket.com.au

Boccaccio Cellars

Excellent selection of Italian wines and special ingredients, including *baccalà* and an array of cured meats, cheeses and more in Melbourne.

boccaccio.com.au

Essential Ingredient	Specialty food and cookware store where you can order online or shop in person (in Victoria, New South Wales and Canberra) for ingredients such as spices, olive oils, pickles and other preserved foods, plus harder-to-find ingredients such as squid ink and white polenta (cornmeal). essentialingredient.com.au
Paesanella	For a mind-boggling range of imported Italian cheeses and local Italian-style cheeses in Sydney's Marrickville, plus numerous other Italian ingredients. paesanella.com.au

In the United Kingdom

Brindisa	A Spanish specialty shop at the Borough Markets and online, where you'll be able to find *baccalà* and squid ink. brindisa.com
Steve Hatt	Historic Islington fishmongers for sustainable fresh seafood and preserved fish. stevehattfishmongers.co.uk
Moxon's	London fishmonger for fresh and in-house smoked fish, plus a good selection of quality pantry items, from squid ink to creamed horseradish. moxonsfreshfish.com
The Fish Society	Online fishmonger where you'll be able to find dried stockfish, *baccalà*, both salted and already desalted (pre-soaked), baby octopus, smoked herring (kippers), whole and peeled brown shrimp (similar to *schie*) and more. thefishsociety.co.uk
Natoora	For seasonal, fresh heirloom Italian produce. You can even find Venetian produce such as Castelfranco and Treviso radicchio. They have shops in various London locations and also online via Ocado. natoora.co.uk

Nanona	Italian food importers based near Bristol with fresh produce, cured meats and cheeses, and pantry ingredients such as 'fioretto' polenta (cornmeal). nanona.co.uk
Valvona & Crolla	Scotland's oldest Italian delicatessen with a huge range of fine ingredients, including cured meats and *baccalà*. valvonacrolla.co.uk

In the United States

Olsen Fish Company	Minneapolis-based supplier of Scandinavian specialty food products including the highest-grade stockfish direct from Norway. olsenfish.com
LaRuche Imports	This self-named 'Best Stockfish Supplier in the USA' in Houston have a sample pack of Norwegian stockfish already cut into pieces (which is handy) for those just wanting to dip their toes in, or whole/scored bigger family and dealer packs for committed stockfish lovers. larucheimports.com
Natoora	Like their UK branch, here you can get strictly seasonal, heirloom produce and rare varieties such as Castelfranco and pink radicchio direct from the Veneto or white peaches from Campania (perfect for those Bellinis). Based in Brooklyn. natoora.com
Barney Greengrass	Historic New York Jewish deli that you could find useful for ingredients such as smoked fish, fresh horseradish and herring. barneygreengrass.com

In Venice and nearby

The Rialto market	The place to shop for food in Venice for the past thousand years. Find stalls of fresh produce by the Grand Canal, plus two undercover *pescherie* housing the fish markets and additional shops such as the ones mentioned below. All around the Rialto you'll find the most typical *bàcari*, wine bars, for sampling *cicchetti* after a shopping trip.
Antica Drogheria Mascari	Near the Rialto market, this old-school shop is the go-to for wine but also for preserves such as mostarda and dried fruit, nuts and an impressive range of spices (could this be what remains of Venice's roaring spice trade?). imascari.com
Casa del Parmigiano	As its name suggests, this is a small and wonderful shop for cheese in the Rialto market. casadelparmigiano.ve.it
I Sapori di Sant'Erasmo	A family-run farm with an on-site shop (and delivery) on the island of Sant'Erasmo for produce grown right in the Venetian lagoon, in particular the tiny artichokes known as *castraure*. isaporidisanterasmo.com
Gastronomia Ortis	An old-school convenience store in Venice's Castello neighbourhood, where you can order and buy *baccalà* (that is, dried stockfish) already soaked in large wooden barrels. You can also buy their in-house *baccalà mantecato*. gastronomiaortis1914.com
Casa del Baccalà	In the historical centre of the town of Treviso, this specialised, family-run *baccalà* shop sells the highest-quality stockfish, including already soaked stockfish, and *baccalà* (salted cod) as well as a variety of ready-made dishes, such as *alla Vicentina, mantecato* and in tomato sauce.

Eating and drinking in Venice – a brief guide

This is a collection of the many wonderful places to eat and drink like a Venetian that inspired the selection of *cicchetti* and treats in this book:

All'Antica Mola (Cannaregio),
see page 76

All'Arco (San Polo),
see page 35

Al Mascaron (Castello),
see page 58

Al Vecchio Marina (Lido di Jesolo),
see page 104

Anice Stellato (Cannaregio),
see page 214

Bancogiro (San Polo),
see page 50

Bar ai Nomboli (San Polo),
see page 94

Bar alla Toletta (Dorsoduro),
see page 94

Bar Rialto da Lollo (San Polo),
see page 94

Bar Tiziano (Cannaregio),
see page 94

Ca' d'oro Alla Vedova (Cannaregio),
see pages 130–131

Caffé Florian (Piazza San Marco),
see pages 18, 130, 197

Cantina del Vino già Schiavi
(or Cantinone) (Dorsoduro),
see pages 35, 106, 156

Cantina Do Mori (San Polo),
see pages 35, 62

Cantina Do Spade (San Polo),
see pages 126, 210

Cantina Aziende Agricole (Cannaregio),
see page 103

Harry's Bar (San Marco),
see pages 172, 193

Rosa Salva in Campo Santi Giovanni
e Paolo (San Marco),
see page 94

Taverna Tipica Veneziana (Torcello),
see page 73

Venissa (Mazzorbo),
see pages 25, 87–89, 153

A map of Venice

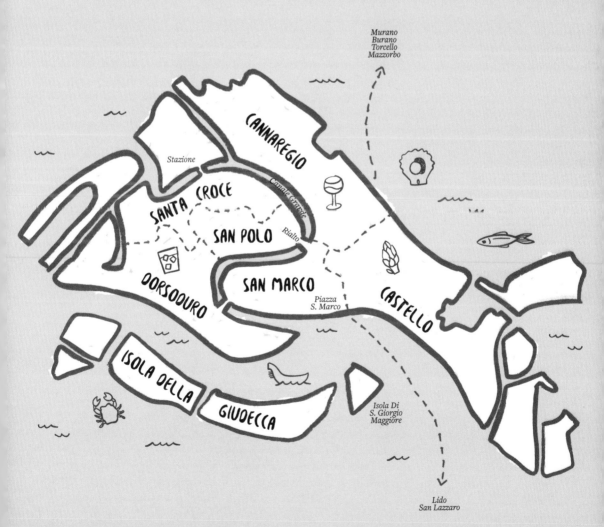

Murano
Burano
Torcello
Mazzorbo

CANNAREGIO

Stazione

Canale Grande

SANTA CROCE

SAN POLO

Rialto

DORSODURO

SAN MARCO

Piazza
S. Marco

CASTELLO

ISOLA DELLA

GIUDECCA

Isola Di
S. Giorgio
Maggiore

Lido
San Lazzaro

Index

References

These are the books that helped me most in understanding the rich history of Venice in relation to its cuisine, as well as a number of wonderful cookbooks both in English and Italian (and even in Venetian dialect) that offer more inspiring Venetian recipes.

Accademia Italiana della Cucina, 2009, *La Cucina: The Regional Cooking of Italy*, Rizzoli, New York.

Artusi, Pellegrino, 1960, *La Scienza in Cucina e l'Arte di Mangiar Bene*, Giunti Marzocco, Florence.

Bellina, Luisa and Mimmo Cappellaro, 1992, *Ricette di Osterie del Veneto: Quaresime e Oriente*, Slow Food Editore, Farigliano.

Boni, Ada, 1994, *Italian Regional Cooking*, Crescent Books, New York.

Brandolisio, Sandro, 2019, *Cichéti: Ricettario dei cichéti preparati nei 'Bàcari' veneziani negli anni '50–'60*, Franco Filippi Editore, Venice.

Coco, Carla, 2009, *Venezia in Cucina*, Editori Laterza, Bari.

Conti, Mila, 2010, *I Sapori del Veneto Cucina Regionale*, RL Libri, Milan.

David, Elizabeth, 2009, *An Omelette and a Glass of Wine*, Grub Street, London.

Del Conte, Anna, 2017, *Classic Food of Northern Italy*, Pavillion Books, London.

Dickie, John, 2007, *Delizia! The Epic History of the Italians and Their Food*, Sceptre, London.

Field, Carol, 1985, *The Italian Baker*, resissue edition, Harper & Rowe, New York.

Kiros, Tessa, 2008, *Venezia: Food and Dreams*, Murdoch Books, Sydney.

McAlpine, Skye, 2018, *A Table in Venice*, Bloomsbury Publishing, London.

Morris, Jan, 1960, *Venice*, Faber and Faber, London.

Necchio, Valeria, 2017, *Veneto: Recipes from an Italian Country Kitchen*, Guardian Faber Publishing, London.

Riley, Gillian, 2009, *The Oxford Companion to Italian Food*, Oxford University Press, New York.

Rorato, Giampiero, 2010, *Origini e Storia della Cucina Veneziana*, Grafiche De Bastiani, Godega di Sant'Urbano.

Rorato, Giampiero, 2015, *Spezie, Vino, Pane della Serenissima*, Dario De Bastiani Editore, Vittorio Veneto.

Salvatori de Zuliani, Mariù, 2001, *A Tola Co I Nostri Veci*, 17th edition, FrancoAngeli, Milan.

Servi, Edda Machlin, 1981, *The Classic Cuisine of the Italian Jews: Traditional Recipes and Menus and a Memoir of a Vanished Way of Life*, Everest House, New York.

Stefani, Mario and Nino Agostinelli, 1978, *Osterie a Venezia*, Edizioni del Lombardo, Padova.

Zompini, Gaetano, 2009, *Le Arti che Vanno per Via*, Filippi Editore Venezia, Venice.

Zorzi, Elio, 2009, *Osterie Veneziane*, Filippi Editore Venezia, IV Edizione, Venice.

Grazie

Writing and photographing this cookbook alone during more than one lockdown was certainly a solitary experience quite different to making my other books, but I am never truly alone in the endeavour. On the contrary, I couldn't have done this without the help of so many people.

Thank you first and foremost to my friend, historian Rosa Salzberg, who had the idea in the first place to make a book about *cicchetti* and their history, and who graciously gave me her blessing to let me write this but was always there along the way, fact-checking, proofreading and ready to toast with a spritz.

I am also indebted to our friends Edoardo Gamba and Krystina Stermole, who always show me a new perspective of Venice, whether it's in a glass factory or on their boat zipping through the Grand Canal with all our kids in tow, and who pulled strings to get me in touch with Manuel Bagnolo, the last of the *moecanti*, the *moeche* fishing families on the Giudecca. I must also thank Manuel for that foggy day out on his boat, one of the most memorable experiences I've ever had, eating the best fried soft-shell crabs of my life.

A special grazie to my inspiring friends Valeria Necchio and Zaira Zarotti for allowing me to include their recipes for *zaleti* and *pan del doge*, respectively, not to mention just enjoying Venice with them is an enormous pleasure.

Thank you to the enthusiastic recipe testers who put their hands up to try some of the recipes before they went into their editing stage. This is such an important part of the making of the book for me; it's the test run, the moment I get to see how the recipes read and how they translate in ordinary homes and to get the valuable feedback before everything goes into print. Thank you (and your families) from the bottom of my heart: Jodie Anderson, Mandi Baldry, Jill Bernadini, Anne Bright, Raffaella Di Maio, Kate Fanning, Sally Frawley, Nicolette Gallo, Karen Louise George, Phoebe Luton, Michelle Molloy, Giulia Porro, Sara Postorino, Terri Salminen, Gabrielle Schaffner, Suzanne Shier, Stephanie Whidden, Peggy Witter and Sing Yee.

Thank you Katharina Allè Trauttmansforff of Trust & Travel for coordinating a stay in the beautiful Palazzo Ca'nova where some of the recipes in these pages were photographed.

Hana, my sister, who edited more than 700 of my location photographs and hundreds more recipe photographs all the way from Melbourne to get them print-ready (and give them that warm Venetian glow) – thank you, I have no idea what I would have done without you.

And to Jane Willson, my publisher, thank you for letting me create this book, for believing in it from day one and for always standing up for it, in every little detail. I so appreciate it, and all the books we have made together, and I will miss you.

Last but not least thank you to my husband, Marco Lami, for being the best *cicchetti* company and cocktail maker I know, and to my mother-in-law and Mariù and Luna, for being so patient with me during the many months of the making of this book.

About the author

Growing up between Australia, Japan and China, Emiko Davies has spent most of her life living abroad, and since 2005 has called Italy home. After gaining a Bachelor of Fine Art in the US at the Rhode Island School of Design, she arrived in Florence to study art restoration and photography. It was in the Renaissance city that she met her husband, Marco Lami. Emiko's passion for food, photography and history, and Marco's journey as a sommelier, led her to start her eponymous food blog in 2010, exploring regional and historical Italian food and wine, as well as travel tips and musings on family life in Italy.

This is her fifth cookbook. She continues to write about food and travel in Italy on her blog, as well as for other publications such as Food52, Saveur, *Financial Times*, *Gourmet Traveller*, *Condé Nast Traveler* and *Corriere della Sera*'s popular food magazine, *Cook*.

She and Marco live in a Tuscan village with their two daughters, where they dream about opening their own wine bar one day.

Published in 2022 by Hardie Grant Books, an imprint of Hardie Grant Publishing

Hardie Grant Books (Melbourne)
Wurundjeri Country
Building 1, 658 Church Street
Richmond, Victoria 3121

Hardie Grant Books (London)
5th & 6th Floors
52–54 Southwark Street
London SE1 1UN

hardiegrantbooks.com

 A catalogue record for this book is available from the National Library of Australia

NATIONAL
LIBRARY
OF AUSTRALIA

Cinnamon and Salt
ISBN 978 1 74379 731 0

10 9 8 7 6 5 4 3 2 1

Publishing Director: Jane Willson
Project Editor: Loran McDougall
Editor: Andrea O'Connor @ Asterisk & Octopus
Design Manager: Kristin Thomas
Designer: George Saad
Photographer: Emiko Davies
Production Manager: Todd Rechner

FSC
www.fsc.org
MIX
Paper from
responsible sources
FSC® C020056

Colour reproduction by Splitting Image Colour Studio
Printed in China by Leo Paper Products LTD.
The paper this book is printed on is from FSC®-certified forests and other sources. FSC® promotes environmentally responsible, socially beneficial and economically viable management of the world's forests.

Hardie Grant acknowledges the Traditional Owners of the country on which we work, the Wurundjeri people of the Kulin nation and the Gadigal people of the Eora nation, and recognises their continuing connection to the land, waters and culture. We pay our respects to their Elders past and present.